INDETERMINACY AND SOCIETY

INDETERMINACY AND SOCIETY

RUSSELL HARDIN

PRINCETON UNIVERSITY PRESS

PRINCETON AND OXFORD

Published by Princeton University Press, 41 William Street, Princeton, New Jersey, 08540
In the United Kingdom: Princeton University Press, 3 Market Place, Woodstock,
Oxfordshire OX20 1SY

Library of Congress Cataloging-in-Publication data
Hardin, Russell, 1940–
Indeterminacy and society / Russell Hardin.
p. cm.
Includes bibliographical references and index.
ISBN: 0-691-09176-5 (alk. paper)
1. Social interaction. 2. Choice (Psychology) 3. Determinism (Philosophy) 1. Title.

HM1111 .H37 2003
302—dc21   2002042720
British Library Cataloging-in-Publication Data is available
This book has been composed in Goudy
Printed on acid-free paper. ∞

www.pupress.princeton.edu
Printed in the United States of America
10 9 8 7 6 5 4 3 2 1

For Brian M. Barry

SPLENDID COLLEAGUE AND CRITIC

FOR THREE DECADES

CONTENTS

PREFACE

THE GENERAL THESIS of this book is that problems of indeterminacy in social interaction are important, pervasive, and often intractable and that they often afflict social theories. I focus on very important major theories or schools of theory because if these have problems that are commonly neglected, then we should become much more alert to indeterminacy and its implications. Often, contributors to these theories seem to be bothered by the indeterminacies that they face and sometimes they address them head on. In a few cases, they assert the centrality of indeterminacies, and their theories therefore openly include assumptions or conclusions of indeterminacy. It is possibly an exaggeration to say that many of the devices used in various theories are provoked by at least an implicit recognition of indeterminacy, but it is also instructive to treat those devices as, indeed, dodges of indeterminacy, whether deliberately conceived that way or not. That is how I will treat them in this book in order to focus attention on the issue of indeterminacy.

The kind of indeterminacy at issue throughout the discussions here is that which often follows from strategic interaction. In strategic interactions I choose a strategy, not an outcome, but I choose it in the hope that it will get me to a desirable outcome. There are strategic interactions, such as pure coordination interactions, in which there is little or no indeterminacy from choosing a strategy rather than directly choosing an outcome. But for the general case of complex interactions between two or more choosers, indeterminacy is a major problem. A partially related form of indeterminacy is that which arises from stochastic problems in which my action (or our actions) lead to a probabilistic array of possible outcomes, as though I were interacting with nature to produce a final outcome from the combination of my strategy choice and nature's. Both of these classes of problem—interactive choice and choice against nature in stochastic contexts—make the simple notion of an action, as commonly treated in the vernacular and in philosophical action theory, very complex because my action commonly does not determine an outcome. My concern is not the details of various theories or even the explication of those theories in general but only with elements of indeterminacy that affect them.

Chapter 2 includes the only technically difficult arguments in the book, and they are not very difficult. But readers may skip chapter 2 or can at least get the brunt of the argument by simply skimming the opening and concluding sections of that chapter.

ACKNOWLEDGMENTS

FOR CONSTRUCTIVE COMMENTS on earlier versions of some parts of this, I wish to thank Ruth Adams, Nomy Arpaly, Paul Bullen, Thomas Christiano, Ed Curley, Arthur Cyr, Jon Elster, James Fearon, Robert Goodin, Geoffrey Keene, Ellen Frankel Paul, Philip Pettit, Richard Posner, Ekkehart Schlicht, Bart Schultz, Rogers Smith, Stephen Stigler, and an anonymous philosopher who thinks anyone who plays the prisoner's dilemma is a criminal. I also wish to thank many participants in the following events: the Bowling Green conference on Foundations of Moral and Political Philosophy; a colloquium of the Institute for Philosophy and Public Policy at the University of Maryland; a panel of the meetings of the American Political Science Association (1992); the legal theory workshop at the Chicago Kent School of Law; the Yale Law School legal theory workshop; a seminar of the Center for the Study of Public Choice, George Mason University; a colloquium in the Philosophy Department in the Faculty of Arts of the Australian National University; a speakers series "The Future for Peace" at the College of Notre Dame of Maryland; several sessions of my informal workshop on contemporary moral and political theory at the University of Chicago; a seminar of the Lawyers Alliance for Nuclear Arms Control in Chicago; a seminar of the Chicago Council on Foreign Relations; and a conference on legal norms at the University of Pennsylvania School of Law. For a unique opportunity to present the entire project, I thank the Rationality on Friday seminar of the Center for Rationality and Interactive Decision Making of the Hebrew University of Jerusalem and its participants. I also thank Nomy Arpaly, Brian Barry, Christopher Morris, Eric Posner, Stephen Stigler, and an anonymous reviewer for Princeton University Press for their commentaries on the entire manuscript. If the book has any felicities or merits, these may be taken as evidence that stochastic processes can be beneficial. I also wish to thank Paul Bullen and Huan Wang for research assistance beyond the call of duty, and New York University, Stanford University, the University of Chicago, the Australian National University, the Andrew W. Mellon Foundation, and the Russell Sage Foundation for support during the writing of this work at its various stages.

Chapter 1 draws in small part on "Difficulties in the Notion of Economic Rationality," *Social Science Information* 23 (1984): 453–467.

Chapter 2 draws in part on "Determinacy and Rational Choice," pp. 191–200 in Reinhard Selten, ed., *Rational Interaction: Essays in Honor of*

John C. Harsanyi (Berlin: Springer-Verlag, 1992), "Contracts, Promises and Arms Control," *Bulletin of the Atomic Scientists* (October 1984): 14–17; and "A Rejoinder" (to Richard B. Bilder), *Bulletin of the Atomic Scientists* (April 1985): 53–54.

Chapter 5 draws on parts of "Magic on the Frontier: The Norm of Efficiency," *University of Pennsylvania Law Review* 144 (May 1996): 1987–2020; chapters 3 and 4 also draw very slightly on this article.

Chapter 6 draws heavily on "Ethics and Stochastic Processes," *Social Philosophy and Policy* 7 (Autumn 1989): 69–80.

Chapters 7 and 8 draw on "Distributive Justice in a Real World," pp. 9–24 in Leo Montada and Melvin Lerner, eds., *Current Social Concerns about Justice* (New York: Plenum, 1996).

I wish to thank the editors and publishers of these journals and books for permission to use the relevant material in substantially modified forms here.

INDETERMINACY AND SOCIETY

Chapter One

Indeterminacy

INDETERMINACY in contexts of strategic interaction—which is to say, in virtually all social contexts—is an issue that is constantly swept under the rug because it is often disruptive to pristine social theory. But the theory is fake: the indeterminacy is real. I wish here to address such indeterminacy, its implications for collective choice, and the ways in which it has been hidden from view or ignored in manifold theories, and some ways in which it has been well handled and even made central to theory. The effort to pretend indeterminacy away or to hide it from view pervades social theory of virtually every kind, from the most technical game-theoretic accounts of extremely fine points to moral theory from its beginnings. The issue is that the basic rationality that makes sense of or fits individual choice in the simplest contexts of choosing against nature does not readily generalize to contexts in which individuals are interacting with other individuals. The basic rationality that says more resources are preferable to less is indeterminate for the more complicated context, which is almost the whole of our lives outside the casino and the lottery.

Typically, the central task in strategic interactions is obtaining the best possible outcome for oneself. Unfortunately, in many social contexts I cannot simply act in a way that determines my own outcome. I can choose only a strategy, not an outcome. All that I determine with my strategy choice is some constraints on the possible array of outcomes I might get. To narrow this array to a single outcome requires action from you and perhaps many others. I commonly cannot know what is the best strategy choice for me to make unless I know what strategy choices others will make. But if all of us can know what all others are going to do, then it is not coherent to say that thereafter we can alter our choices in the light of that knowledge. This is the form of indeterminacy at issue in this book: *indeterminacy that results from strategic interaction.* Interactive choice as represented descriptively in game theory is often indeterminate for each individual chooser. For an individual chooser in a moment of choice, this indeterminacy is not a failure of reason by the chooser; the indeterminacy is in the world because it follows from the mismatch of the preferences of all those in the interaction of the moment.

Problems of a partially related kind were characterized by C. H. Waddington ([1960] 1967, 17), in a sadly neglected book, as *stochastic.* This word, which means, roughly, "probabilistic," comes from a Greek root that means "proceed-ing by guesswork" or, more literally, "skillful in aiming." Stochastic problems are those for which, in a sense, nature might outsmart our choice of strategy so that we get an outcome very different from what we would have wanted, at least in some cases. As a remarkably clear and varied example of the problems at issue, I will often discuss problems of vaccination against a major disease. That range of problems has the attractive feature that it, in its simpler forms, should not be very controversial, either pragmatically, causally, or morally. Especially because it is often not morally controversial, it will be very useful in exemplifying the nature of stochastic policy problems, including many, such as nuclear deterrence (in which accidents could have happened), that are also troubled with strategic interaction. For stochastic problems of individual choice, we can readily reduce our choices to their expected values; and then we can select more rather than less. Stochastic collective choices or policies commonly entail losses for some and gains for others, so that we can choose unproblematically from expected value only if we do not know in advance who will be the losers and gainers.

To see the peculiarly stochastic nature of many collective choice problems that we face, consider the program of polio vaccination before it was eradicated as a disease in the wild in North America (that is, outside certain laboratory stores of the virus). The facts are roughly these. We vaccinate millions, includ-ing almost the entire population of children. Many of these would die and many would be permanently, even hideously, crippled if not vaccinated. Among those vaccinated, a very small number suffer serious cases of paralytic polio. There is no question that fewer are harmed by vaccinating than by not vaccinating the population. Our strategic action is to protect people, but among the outcomes that could follow from our action, we also harm some people, some of whom might never have got polio if not vaccinated or even if no one had been vaccinated.[1]

When we choose an action or a policy, this is often the structure of it. We have some chance of doing harm and some chance of doing good in the un-avoidable sense that in order to do something good we must risk doing some-thing bad. Sometimes this is for reasons of the nature of the world, as in the case of vaccination. But at other times it is for reasons of the nature of strategic interaction. I choose, in a sense, a strategy, not an outcome. Then I get an outcome that is the result of the strategy choices of others in interaction with my choice.

These two classes of problems, strategic interaction and stochastic patterns of outcomes, have a common feature, which is the central issue of this book. They make indeterminate what an action or a policy is. In philosophical action theory, the actions are simple ones such as flipping a switch to turn on a light. In real life, our most important actions are not so simple. They are inherently interactions. We have reasons for taking our actions, but our reasons may not finally be reflected in the results of our actions even if hope for specific results is our reason for our choice of actions.

In three contexts I argue that taking indeterminacy into account up front by making it an assumption helps us to analyze certain problems correctly or to resolve them successfully. In these cases, using theories that ignore the indeterminacy at issue can lead to clouded understandings, even wrong understandings of the relevant issues. One of these contexts is the hoary problem of the iterated prisoner's dilemma and what strategy is rational when playing it. The second is the real world prisoner's dilemma of nuclear deterrence policy that, one hopes, is now past. The third is the great classical problem of how we can justify institutional actions that violate honored principles. For example, public policy is often determined by a cost-benefit analysis, which entails interpersonal comparisons of utility. The people who do these policy analyses are commonly economists who eschew interpersonal comparisons as metaphysically meaningless. Such comparisons are one theoretical device for avoiding indeterminacy. Although they have been intellectually rejected on theoretical grounds, and seemingly rightly so, still they make eminently good sense on an account of their authorization that is grounded in indeterminacy. In all three of these contexts, by starting with the—correct—presumption of indeterminacy, we get to a better outcome than if we insist on imposing determinacy.

Note that the vaccination case, in which some are harmed while others are benefited, is only a partial or reduced analogue of the social interaction case in which depending on what you do, I may do very well or very badly. The problem is simplified in that one of the actors is nature, rather than a strategically manipulative agent with its own interests possibly in conflict with ours. Keeping this simplified problem in mind helps to make the more complex issues of strategic interaction between two or more manipulative, self-interested agents relatively clear. The causal analysis of stochastic problems such as vaccination policy is unlikely to be controversial, whereas any account of a strategic interaction that stipulates what each of the parties will do or ought to do is likely to be controversial. Indeed, that is the central fact that provokes this work.

Strategic Interaction

It is a correct assessment of rationality in social contexts that it is ill defined and often indeterminate. If this is true, then any instruction on what it is rational to do should not be based on the (wrong) assumption of determinacy. Assuming that the world of social choice is indeterminate rather than determinate would lead one to make different decisions in many contexts. Determinacy can be both disabling and enabling, depending on the nature of the decisions at stake. The indeterminacy of a principle of rational choice sometimes plays into the indeterminacy of knowledge, but I wish to address problems of knowledge primarily as they affect rational choice through strategic or rational indeterminacy, not as they affect ordinary decision making through epistemological indeterminacy.

Epistemological indeterminacy from causal ignorance—for example, from inadequate theory or inadequate knowledge—is a major problem in its own right, but it is not the focus here. Hence, I am not concerned with the disruptive possibilities of unintended consequences (which are a major problem in innovation and in public policy), even insofar as they result from complex interactions.

Strategic or rational indeterminacy, as in current theory, is partly the product of the ordinal revolution in economic and choice theory. That revolution has swept up economics and utilitarianism and has helped spawn rational choice theory through the ordinal theories of Kenneth Arrow ([1951] 1963) and Joseph Schumpeter ([1942] 1950). The problem of such indeterminacy arises from simple aggregation of interests, and therefore it is pervasive in neoclassical economics as well as in ordinal utilitarianism or welfarism. It is pervasive *because our choices have social (or interactive) contexts*. Arrow demonstrated this indeterminacy in principle already in one of the founding works of social choice. It is instructive that he discovered the indeterminacy while trying to find a determinate solution to collective aggregation of ordinal preferences. Unlike most theorists, however, he did not quail from the discovery but made it the center piece of his Impossibility Theorem (Arrow 1983, 1–4).

Because there is collective indeterminacy, there is indeterminacy in individual choice in contexts of strategic interaction. These are, in a sense, contexts of aggregation of interests, even though there may be substantial conflict over how to aggregate and those in interaction need not be concerned at all with the aggregate but only with personal outcomes. In such interactions, we may treat each other as merely part of the furniture of the universe with which we have to deal, so that we have no direct concern with the aggregate outcome, only with our own. As John Rawls (1999, 112 [1971, 128]) supposes, we are mutually disinterested. We should finally see such indeterminacy not as an anomaly but as the normal state of affairs, on which theory should build. Theory that runs afoul of such indeterminacy is often foul theory.

A quick survey of contexts of strategic interaction in which indeterminacy has played an important role and in which theorists have attempted to get around it or to deal with it would include at least the following seven (each of these will be discussed more fully in later chapters).

In game theory, John Harsanyi simply stipulates that a solution theory must be determinate despite the fact that adopting his determinacy principle makes no sense as an optimizing move. His move comes from nowhere, as though somehow it is irrational to live with indeterminacy (in which case it is irrational to live). It appears to be a response to the oddity of the prisoner's dilemma game when this game is iterated for a fixed number of plays (see chapter 2).

That game is a pervasive part of life because it is essentially the structure of exchange. Any economist's theory of rationality must be able to handle that game. One might even say that the analysis of that game should come before almost anything else in the economist's world.

Equilibrium theory in economics is fundamentally indeterminate if there is a coordination problem. There is a coordination problem whenever there is more than one coordination equilibrium. In any whole economy, to which general equilibrium is meant to apply, there are apt to be numerous coordination problems in the abstract (see chapter 2).

Thomas Hobbes attempted to trick up determinacy in his theory of the creation of a sovereign, although he needed no trickery in his selection of any extant sovereign as determinately preferable to putting any alternative in place by rebellion (see chapter 3).

Jeremy Bentham imposed determinacy in his version of utilitarianism by supposing that utilities are comparable and additive across persons, so that in a comparison of various states of the universe, we could supposedly add up the utilities and immediately discover which state has the highest utility (see chapter 4).

Ronald Coase, with his Coase Theorem, may have made the cleverest move to overcome the problem of indeterminacy in an ordinal world by using cardinal prices to resolve the choice of what to produce (see chapter 5), although his resolution of this problem still leaves open the question of how to share the gains from production among the owners of the relevant productive assets.

A standard move in much of moral theory is to reduce the inordinate multiplicity of possible problems of individual choice by introducing a set of rules that grossly simplifies the choices we must make (see chapter 6). Such moral theory is now called deontology.

In his theory of justice, John Rawls achieves the appearance of determinacy in the abstract with his difference principle, but under that appearance there is a morass of indeterminacy in his category of primary goods that, if taken seriously, negates much of the seeming simplicity and appeal of his theory (see chapter 7). Nevertheless, far more clearly than most of the theorists considered here, he recognizes the centrality of the problem of indeterminacy in social choice and very cleverly attempts to overcome it.

We may ex ante create institutions that make decisions on principles that we would not have been able to use directly. For example, it may be mutually advantageous ex ante for us to have an institution use cost-benefit analysis, with its attendant interpersonal comparisons, even though we might not be able to give a mutual-advantage defense of such an analysis in any particular instance of its application (see chapter 8).

The responses to these contexts include three failures of theory: to ignore the problem and suppose that choice theory is determinate (as in Harsanyi's game theory and in equilibrium theory); to cardinalize the values at issue so that they can then be added up in various states and the highest value can be selected (as in Bentham's utilitarianism); and to adopt very limited but relatively precise rules or principles for behavior that cover some limited range of things and to exempt other things from coverage (as in deontological ethics).

There are three pragmatic responses that are variously effective: to simplify the problem so that ordinal resolution is relatively determinate (as in the moves of Hobbes and Rawls, as discussed in chapters 3 and 7); to keep everything ordinal and noncomparable up to the point of comparing the cardinal market values of what is produced (as in Coase's theorem in chapter 5); and to shift the burden of choice to an institution to achieve mechanical determinacy (as discussed in chapter 8).

Finally, there is also the possibility of accepting indeterminacy and resolving issues by making indeterminacy an assumption or conclusion of the analysis, as in Arrow's theorem, rather than a problem to be ignored or attended to later.

Each of these responses yields determinate solutions to problems up to the limit of the device. The first three devices, however, block out of view the fundamental indeterminacy of the choice or assessment problem. And the three pragmatic devices may obscure the underlying indeterminacy. I will discuss these six devices in subsequent chapters. Shifting the burden of choice ex ante to an institution is in part the resolution of Hobbes and Rawls, but it is more substantially the way we handle public policies in the face of the other, generally less workable resolutions in the list. The last way of dealing with indeterminacy—simply to face it and incorporate it into analysis—is, so far, not very common. I think it yields a correct analysis of social choice in an ordinal world in Arrow's Impossibility Theorem, a finally correct analysis of how to play in iterated prisoner's dilemma (which is a good model of much of the life of exchange and cooperation), a credible and effective account of how to handle such issues as nuclear arms control, and the richest and most compelling vision of social order that we know. It also leads Rawls to his difference principle for handling plural values. It additionally fits many other problems and theories that will not be addressed here, including general solution theories for games,[2] the size or minimum-winning coalition theory of William Riker (1962; Hardin 1976), chaos theory in electoral choice (Mueller 1989), and many others.

The varied ways of dealing with indeterminacy have distinctively different realms of application, as briefly noted above and as I will discuss further in later chapters. For example, Hobbes's grand simplification of the problem of social order allowed him to conclude that any stable government is better than none and that loyalty to any extant government is better than any attempt to put a better one in its place. But it also works in some cases in which simplification of the interests at stake is not even necessary. Coase's resolution is of marginal problems of allocating resources for production. It arises as a problem only after Hobbes's or some other resolution of the general problem of social order has been achieved. Cardinalization with interpersonal comparisons of welfare would work at any level, from foundational to marginal, if it could be made intelligible, as sometimes perhaps it can be. At the very least, we frequently act as though it makes sense, often in fundamentally important contexts, such as in many public policy decisions.

The first three of these devices are efforts to trick out as much as possible from what indeterminacy there may be. When any of them works, it is fine, although many people, especially including economists, reject any appeal to interpersonal comparison of welfare as meaningless. But the devices do not always work very well, and then we are left with trying to deal with indeterminacy or trying to trick ourselves, rather than the world, into believing, for example, that a limited set of moral rules can be adequate for at least morality. The responses are of quite different kinds, and there have probably been other devices of significance. Their sophistication and variety suggest how pervasive and varied the problem of indeterminacy is.

By now, one might suppose we would have recognized that indeterminacy is part of the nature of our problems in various contexts. Tricking or fencing it out of the picture is commonly misguided and will not help us resolve or even understand many of our individual and social choice problems, as Arrow clearly understood. Instead of imposing determinate principles on an indeterminate world in some contexts, we should often seek principles that build on the indeterminacy we must master if we are to do well. If we do this, we will most likely find that the principles we apply will be incomplete. They will apply to choices over some ranges of possibilities and not over others.

For many choice contexts, the principle we might adopt is the pragmatic principle of melioration rather than maximization, which is inherently undefinable for many contexts. I will take melioration to be modal advantage, which is expected advantage to all ex ante, although it may commonly happen that not all gain ex post. For social choice and for moral judgment of aggregate outcomes, the principle for which I will argue is, *when it is not indeterminate*, mutual advantage. This principle will often make sense ex ante although not ex post, as will be exemplified in a discussion of vaccination (chapter 3). In actual life, especially in politics, we will more likely see a limited version of it that we might call sociological mutual advantage. Our political arrangements will serve the mutual advantage of groups that have the power to block alternatives and may substantially ignore groups without such power (Hardin 1999d, chap. 1 and passim). Sociological mutual advantage, however, lacks the normative weight of fully inclusive mutual advantage.

When mutual advantage is not decisive and we nevertheless have to decide what to do, we may have recourse to an aggregate variant of melioration in which some interpersonal comparisons might be made. *This is itself a mutual advantage move ex ante*. That is to say, we know in advance that mutual advantage in case-by-case collective decisions will not work. We therefore need a principle for handling those cases. Adopting a relatively loose principle of melioration for handling such cases when they arise can be mutually advantageous even though its specific applications will not be. Even more commonly, we create an institution that will then apply such a meliorative principle, so that we get mechanical determinacy.

The claim for indeterminacy here is not merely another silly metaphor on quantum mechanics. Interactive choice and aggregate valuation just are sometimes indeterminate. This is not an analog or metaphorical extension of indeterminacy in physics. Social indeterminacy is a problem of set-theoretic choice theory rather than of physical possibilities. *The central problem is indeterminacy of reason in the face of strategic interaction.* Terms in the family *rational* often seem to lose their clarity and supposed definitiveness in such contexts. In fact, they are not univocally definitive. Beyond contexts in which basic rationality—to prefer more to less value when nothing else is at stake in the choice—suffices for choice, if we wish to have determinate theory, we must bring in many additional principles that are often ad hoc and that are not as compelling as basic rationality. Stochastic problems are simpler than those of complex strategic interaction. In them, I or we commonly get one from a probabilistic array of possibilities and we cannot narrow the choice to the best possibility in the array, although it might turn out to be the outcome we get. In such choices, we are, in a sense, choosing against nature, who plays her own strategy.

Indeterminacy in strategic interaction has been clearly recognized in certain contexts for more than two centuries. In the era of the French Revolution, the marquis de Condorcet recognized that in the context of majority voting, there can be cyclic majorities in which, say, candidate *A* defeats candidate *B* by a majority, *B* defeats *C* by a different majority, and *C* defeats *A* by yet another majority. Hence, the principle of majority choice is indeterminate. Moreover, at least since Hobbes the problem of indeterminacy has troubled many social theorists, most of whom have attempted to dodge it. Often, the greater part of wisdom is finally to recognize its pervasiveness and to deal with it by grounding our theories in it, not by building pristine, determinate theories and then trying to force social reality to fit these, or even criticizing it for failing to fit.

We often also face causal indeterminacy, which will come into discussion here insofar as it plays a strong role in defining the possible ways of dealing with indeterminacy in strategic or rational choice. Causal indeterminacy might often be merely a lack of adequate understanding of causal relations, so that it might be corrected. Rational or social indeterminacy is not merely a lack of understanding, and it cannot be corrected, although we might find pragmatic dodges or tricks to help us master the problems it creates.

Ordinalism

The principal reason for social indeterminacy is the pluralism of values and evaluators typically involved in social choice. A brief account of ordinalism and its intellectual origins is therefore useful. The clear and explicit understanding of social choice as an ordinal problem began with Vilfredo Pareto's insights that lie behind what are now called the Pareto criteria: Pareto efficiency or optimality and Pareto superiority. A state of affairs Q is Pareto superior to another state P if at least one person is better off in Q than in P and no one is worse off in Q than in P. And a state of affairs Q is Pareto efficient or optimal if there is no other state that is Pareto superior to it. The latter condition implies that any move would make at least one person worse off or would make no one better off.

It seems plausible that, implicitly, ordinal valuations were commonly assumed in many writings long before Pareto. For example, Thomas Hobbes, David Hume, and Adam Smith were generally ordinalists. But the clear focus on ordinalism and the attempt to analyze its implications came as a response to the suppositions, overt in Bentham and often seemingly tacit before Bentham, that utility is cardinal and that utility across persons can be added. That view dominated much of nineteenth-century thought. But cardinalism was a mistaken invention of high theory. The task that Pareto faced was to make systematic sense of ordinalism. That task was finally carried to fruition in the so-called ordinal revolution in economics in the 1930s (see Samuelson 1974). The implausibility of cardinal, additive utility was already problematic for understanding how prices could vary. The marginal revolution of the nineteenth century was half of the mastery of that problem; the mastery was completed in the ordinal revolution.

The ordinal Pareto criteria are commonly treated as though they were rationally not problematic. But they are subject to strategic problems in practice if they are taken to imply recommendations for action. Unfortunately, the Pareto criteria are about valuations of the states of affairs, and the valuations do not guarantee the actions—exchanges—that would bring us to those states. Moves to Pareto superior states are often thought to be rational because everyone will consent to them because there will be no losers, only gainers, from such moves. But some might not consent. Why? Because any move will not merely determine a present improvement but also will determine what states will be reachable from the newly reached state. Doing especially well—compared to others—on the first move raises the floor from which one maneuvers for the next and subsequent moves. Doing badly on the first move, while nevertheless benefiting at least somewhat in comparison to one's status quo point, lowers the ceiling to which one can aspire on later moves. Figure 1.1 shows this point more clearly.

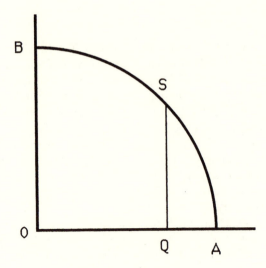

Fig 1.1. Pareto frontier

Figure 1.1 represents a distribution of resources between *A* and *B* beginning from the initial or status quo distribution at the origin, 0. The Pareto frontier represents the set of distributions that are Pareto optimal and also Pareto superior to the status quo. We can imagine that *A* and *B* have holdings of various goods at the status quo distribution and that, through exchange, they can both be made better off. When they reach a stage at which no further voluntary exchanges can be made, they will be at some point on the frontier, represented by the arc from *A* to *B*. On the frontier, any move or exchange that would make *A* better off would make *B* worse off. Any point between the origin and the frontier is accessible from the origin with a Pareto-superior move. For example, the move from the origin to the point *Q* (inside the frontier) makes *A* better off without affecting *B*'s welfare. A move from *Q* back to 0, however, is not a Pareto-superior move because it reduces the welfare of *A*. But note what a move from 0 to *Q* does. It effectively defines a new Pareto frontier that includes all points of the original frontier (from *A* to *S*) that are not to the left of *Q*. All of the points that have been eliminated (all those from *B* to *S*) would be preferred by *B* to any of the points that remain, while all of those that remain would be preferred by *A* to any that have been eliminated. In a meaningful sense, *A* has gained while *B* has lost in the move from 0 to *Q*. *B*'s loss could be called an opportunity cost.

Why then should we say it is rational for *B* to consent to the Pareto-superior move from 0 to *Q*? It is self-evidently rational for *B* to consent to the move *only if* it excludes no points that *B* would prefer to the remaining Pareto-superior points. This will be true if the move from 0 to *Q* is in the only direction in which it is possible to move. But this just means that the Pareto frontier must not be a curve as drawn in figure 1, but must be a point directly to the right of the origin. If the Pareto frontier is as drawn in figure 1, B cannot rationally consent to any move without first considering its effect on an eventual Pareto-optimal distribution. Hence, Pareto superiority is not a criterion for rational choice.

If I am narrowly rational, I can be indifferent to what you gain from a trade from me only if it does not potentially restrict what I can gain from further trades with you. For A and B in the situation of figure 1, however, every Pareto-superior move involves opportunity costs for at least one of the two and often for both of them. That is to say, the move eliminates some attractive opportunities from the field of subsequent choice.[3] Hence, one cannot view the criterion of Pareto superiority as a principle of rational choice in general. The criterion is rationally objectionable because it presumes consent in situations in which conflict can arise over potential allocations. Because my future opportunities may depend on how we allocate things now, my interests now depend on my future prospects.

The Pareto criteria are commonly indeterminate in judging pairs of outcomes even if these problems do not afflict them. For example, any two points on the frontier are Pareto noncomparable. We cannot say that either of these states of affairs is Pareto superior to the other. If opportunity costs are taken into account, we may further not be able to say that any pair of states of affairs is Pareto comparable, with one state superior to the other. Alas, therefore, the Pareto principles reintroduce indeterminacy if they are taken to recommend action.

Pareto combined Hobbes's normative principle of mutual advantage with marginalist concern. Indeed, Pareto ([1927] 1971, 47–51) formulated his principles to avoid interpersonal comparisons and attendant moral judgments. Hence, Pareto was Hobbesian in his motivations, at least in part. The criteria were introduced by Pareto not for recommending individual action but for making ordinal value judgments about states of affairs. They might therefore be used by a policy maker.

The Pareto principles are static principles about the distribution of those goods we already have. They are not dynamic or production-oriented. In this respect, they might seem to be an aberration, as is Benthamite additive utility if it is to be done with precision. But the Paretian analysis of static efficiency accounts for a real issue and is therefore not merely an aberration. It may nevertheless often be largely beside the point for our purposes, although it comes back in through Coasean efficiency in law and economics. The indeterminacy of the notion of Pareto improvement is in the allocation of some surplus available to us beyond the status quo. Most allocations of the surplus might make every one of us better off and would, therefore, be mutually advantageous.[4]

MUTUAL ADVANTAGE: THE COLLECTIVE IMPLICATION OF SELF-INTEREST

During the century or two ending about 1900, microeconomics and utilitarianism developed together. At the beginning of the twentieth century G. E. Moore was the first major utilitarian philosopher who did not also write on economics; indeed, economists might not be surprised to learn that he mangled value theory and therewith utilitarianism. His value theory reverted to the crude notion that some value inheres in objects independently of anyone's use of or pleasure in those objects (Moore 1903, 84). A variant of this notion lies behind the labor theory of value, according to which the value of the object is the quantity of total labor time for producing it—the Salieri theory of value.[5] John Stuart Mill and Henry Sidgwick, the great nineteenth-century utilitarians, both wrote treatises on economics, and much of what they say about value theory is grounded in their economic understandings. Moore returned speculation on value to the Platonic mode of pure reason, so called.

It is ironic that many of the outstanding problems in economic value theory were resolved in Moore's time by Pareto, as will be discussed in chapter 3, and the exponents of the ordinal revolution who followed his lead in the 1930s. Moore was evidently oblivious of these developments. Major economists of Moore's time were avowedly utilitarian (Edgeworth 1881; Pigou [1920] 1932), yet intellectually they had little in common with Moore. Moore's one great insight into value theory—that the value of a whole is not a simple addition of the values of its parts—is one of the problems that stimulated the ordinal revolution and that was resolved by it (see Hardin 1988, 7; Moore 1906, 28). That insight was not entirely original with Moore. Mill had earlier referred to the analogous issue in objective causal contexts as a matter of "chemical" combinations, because when two chemicals are brought together, the result is commonly a chemical reaction that produces a compound with none of the distinctive properties of the original chemicals—as combining the two gases hydrogen and oxygen produces water. So too, in value theory, bringing two things together may produce a combined value that is unrelated to the sum of the values of the two things taken separately.

Many (perhaps most) economists in the Anglo-Saxon tradition have continued to be utilitarian insofar as they have a concern with moral theory or normative evaluation. Unfortunately, at the time of Moore, utilitarianism in philosophy separated from economics and therefore from developments in economic value theory—just when these could have helped to reconstruct or continue the intellectual development of utilitarianism. The two traditions have been brought back together most extensively since then in the contemporary movement of law and economics. This rejoining recalls the early origins of the general utilitarian justification of government in the theory of Hobbes. The chief difference is that Hobbes's concern was foundational, whereas the concern of law and economics is marginalist. Hobbes was concerned with establishing social order at all; law and economics focuses on rules for legal allocations in an already well ordered society. In both law and economics and in Hobbes's theory of the sovereign, a principal focus is on normative justification. And in both, the basic principle of normative justification is self-interest somehow generalized to the collective level, as discussed further below.

The distinctive unity of the visions of those I will canvass in the development from Hobbes to Coase is that it is welfarist. But Hobbes, Pareto, and Coase are not part of the Benthamite classical utilitarian aberration in interpersonally additive welfarism. It is therefore perhaps less misleading here to speak of welfare rather than of utility, although the contemporary notion of utility is manifold in its range of meanings. The chief reason for speaking of welfare rather than utility is that the language of welfare is different from that of utility. Typically we do not want *more* welfare, although we often want greater welfare or a higher level of welfare. Welfare is not a cardinal value made up of smaller bits of welfare, as utility is sometimes assumed to be. The language of welfare is typically ordinalist. I will generally refer to utility only in discussing Bentham's views and will otherwise speak of welfare or well-being.

The normative foundations of the formulations of Hobbes, Vilfredo Pareto, and Ronald Coase are essentially the same. Hobbes emphasized that all we have are individual values (essentially the values of self-interest: survival and welfare) and that individuals can be motivated by resolutions of their collective problem only if these speak to their interests. Pareto, writing after a century of Benthamite additive utilitarianism, asserted that we do not know what aggregation of utility across individuals means, that it is a metaphysical notion. Both Hobbes and Pareto concluded that we can ground a motivational theory only in disaggregated individual values. The only collective value that can be directly imputed from these is mutual advantage, in which all gain (Hobbes's usual assumption) or at least none loses while at least one gains (Pareto's assumption).

Coase ([1960] 1988) is less concerned to state his value position than were Hobbes and Pareto, but his position also seems clearly to suppose that collective values are reducible to individual values or that the only values of concern in his accounts are individual values. An example of this move is in Coase's discussion of the negotiations between a rancher and a farmer on the optimizing of returns from their joint enterprises. The total net profits from the farmer's crops and the rancher's cattle are a function of their sales value less the costs of raising them. This total is essentially a cardinal value in, say, dollars. Suppose these profits could be increased by letting the cattle roam over part of the farmer's land, destroying some of her crops, but that the farmer has the right to fence her land against the cattle. The two then have an interest in striking a deal that allows the cattle to roam over part of the farmer's land (Coase [1960]

1988, 95, 99). In this deal, part of the extra profits the rancher makes from the farmer's not fencing his cattle off her land go to the farmer as compensation for lost profits from her damaged crops, and the two split the remaining extra profits. Hence, each can be made ordinally better off by making the deal. In rough terms, this example generalizes as Coase's theorem.

For ordinalists such as Hobbes, Pareto, and Coase, we may say that *mutual advantage is the collective implication of self-interest* because to say that an outcome of our choices is mutually advantageous is to say that it serves the interest of each and every one of us. One could say that, in this view, collective value is emergent; it is merely what individuals want. But one could also say that this is what the value is: to let individual values prevail. To speak of collective value in any other sense is to import some additional notion of value into the discussion beyond the interests of individuals. Hobbes may have been constitutionally oblivious of any such additional notions of value; Pareto evidently believed them perverse.

Incidentally, mutual advantage is the only plausible collective analog of self-interest. Consider a cardinally additive measure, for example. More utility to you can compensate for less utility to me in such an additive measure. Of course, it cannot be my interest for you to benefit at my expense. Hence, a cardinally additive measure is not a collective analog of individual-level self-interest.

CONCLUDING REMARKS

Almost all of the discussions here are welfarist. The indeterminacies have to do with interests and with their aggregation or balancing in some way. In chapter 2, the concern is with the definition of interests. In subsequent chapters, it is more generally with the aggregation or balancing of interests. Sometimes resources come into play, as in discussions of Posner's wealth maximization (chapter 4), Coase's theorem (chapter 5) and Rawls's theory of justice (chapter 7). Sometimes, resources have been invoked as a genuine alternative to welfare for various conceptual reasons, as in their use by Posner and Rawls and in Amartya Sen's (1985, 1999) arguments for capacities as the core concern of political theory. Sometimes they are merely a useful device for dealing with welfare, as in Coase's theorem. In the discussion of moral rules as a device to ignore indeterminacies (chapter 6), welfare and resources are not generally at issue.

Few technical problems in rational choice have been hashed out and fought over as intensely as the analysis of how to play in an iterated prisoner's dilemma (chapter 2). And no problem in all the millennial history of political philosophy has been more central and debated than how to justify government and its actions (chapters 3, 7, and 8). Both these problems are substantially clarified by recognizing that they are indeterminate in important ways, so that our theories for handling them must be grounded in indeterminacy.

The critical success of some theories historically has probably depended substantially on papering over the indeterminacy that undercuts them, as in the case of Locke's contractarianism, more recent variants of arguments from reasonable agreement and deliberative democracy, and Rawls's theory of distributive justice. Despite its flaccidity, Locke's contractarianism has commonly been taken to be a better account of the justification of government than has Hobbes's theory. This judgment is badly wrong. Hobbes achieves the astonishing success of founding government in an account from self-interest, or rather from its collective implication in mutual advantage. Locke's theory leaves us dependent on a normative commitment that is not credible.

There are many related arguments along the way. For example, if rational choice were determinate, then it would tend to produce equilibrium outcomes. But if rationality is indeterminate, equilibrium may also be indeterminate, as I argue it is, if properly conceived, in the iterated prisoner's dilemma (chapter 2). If we do reach equilibrium outcomes, we may generally expect to be stuck with them. But in many contexts there will in general be no reason to expect to reach equilibrium because there will be none. Daily life and political theory lack equilibriums, and we should probably be glad of that—at least if we are welfarist, as we must be to some extent no matter how much we might assert that welfarism is a wrong or bad moral theory. To paraphrase Keynes, at equilibrium, we are all dead—or at least we have stopped all production.

Although I will not argue this claim extensively here, if welfarism is a bad moral theory, then it is also a bad pragmatic theory. But to suppose it a bad pragmatic theory is so utterly implausible that one cannot sensibly hold that it is a bad moral theory. At the very least, it must be a large part of any good moral theory. This is most conspicuously true, perhaps, in the context of designing institutions for our social life.

My purpose in the discussions of the following chapters is not specifically to explicate the relevant theories of, for example, Hobbes, Kant, Bentham, Coase, Rawls, or Posner. I merely address the problems and successes their theories may have with indeterminacy, because it is the significance of indeterminacy in society and in strategic interactions that I wish to understand. The strengths of some of these theories are arguably more impressive than their weaknesses, but I have deliberately focused on one aspect of their weaknesses.

Chapter Two

Beyond Basic Rationality

THE SIMPLEST DEFINITION of rationality, which fits simple problems of choice, is that one should choose more rather than less value. This is basic rationality. It is almost the only principle of rationality that is universally accepted. The only other is that our rankings of possible choices should be transitive. Transitivity is an immediate inference from cardinal values; by inspection, if 4 is greater than 3 and 3 is greater than 2, then 4 is also greater than 2. Even in an ordinal world, there should be a relation of "greater than" or "better than" or "preferred to" that is transitive. Indeed, suppose you intransitively prefer A to B, B to C, and C to A. Now, if you have C, you should be willing to pay a bit to get B for C, then another bit to get A for B, and yet another bit to get C for A, landing you foolishly back where you started but with reduced funds. Hence, we may include transitivity in basic rationality. Our problems in life begin when we find it hard to make sense of basic rationality in more complex contexts of interactive choice.

Suppose we have a fully determinate rational choice theory that will tell each of us what to do in any particular interactive choice context, and suppose each of us knows the positions of all the others. From our theory I can calculate not only what I ought to do, but also what each other agent in the interaction ought rationally to do. If that theory yields determinate solutions, in the sense that it tells each of us explicitly what to do, these solutions must be in equilibrium for rational players who have full knowledge of the payoff structure, who have this theory, and who assume that their co-players are rational and have this theory.

If a purported solution were not in equilibrium, then, by the definition of equilibrium, at least one of the players would have an incentive to choose a different strategy in order to receive a better payoff. But a coherent theory cannot be used against itself to tell me to do other than what it commends. Hence, each of us must find that what the theory tells us to do, if all others are also following the theory, leads to an equilibrium outcome. If it does not do this, the theory is at least partially indeterminate. Rational choice is indeterminate in this sense for some ongoing interactions, such as the iterated prisoner's dilemma, and for the class of moderately complex games or interactive choice contexts, as I will argue here.

John Harsanyi (1956, 1977) has long argued for determinacy in game-theoretic rational choice theory. Not surprisingly, he has also generally argued for equilibrium outcomes as the result of rational choice (Harsanyi and Selten 1988). Against this general position, I wish to argue that primitive notions of rationality do not entail determinacy when followed by all agents to an interaction. Moreover, the simple concept of equilibrium in certain classes of interactions does not generalize in a clear way to more complex classes. Both basic rationality and equilibrium require additional elements if they are to apply to many contexts. The imposition of determinacy might be such an additional element, as Harsanyi suggests. Including it as a part of the notion of rationality, however, is an extrarational move that is not compelling in many contexts. In particular, it is not compelling in contexts, such as iterated prisoner's dilemma, in which our theory must give contingent instructions on how to play into the future. If we find that rationality is indeterminate in this important and analytically very clear case, we must conclude that it is more generally indeterminate.

Basic Rationality

First, focus on the underlying intuition that stands firm through all the problems we may face: A rational person prefers more value to less. If there are no cardinal values, as in dollars, then a rational person has transitive preferences over ordinally ranked outcomes. For example, if I prefer A to B and B to C, then I prefer A to C. For present purposes, I will assume cardinal utility in keeping with the overwhelming practice in game-theoretic discussions until recently, so that we may dispense with reference to transitivity in a strictly ordinal theory of preference. The assumption of cardinality is not necessary, but it simplifies discussion here.

In cardinal contexts, preference for A over B merely means the value of A is greater than the value of B. Many critics of this notion of rationality make the simplistically one-step, materialist mistake of supposing that the notion implies that one should prefer more to less of anything valued at all. But, obviously, I may not prefer more dinner to less tonight because I may not prefer the consequences of still more once I have consumed enough. Indeed, I am unlikely even to have appetite for more beyond some level of consumption. *Cardinal preference for more is strictly preference for more value or utility or resources and is therefore trivially transitive.* Almost no one has difficulty with this claim.[1]

If my preferences are transitive in this cardinal sense, it follows that if I am choosing from a finite number of possibilities, there must be one or more possibilities that I prefer to all others, or that I hold indifferent to all others, so that in this case preferring more to less value is equivalent to maximizing. I choose the largest element in my choice set. Our more general problem is how to choose under varied constraints when we have to compromise with the principle of maximization. An obvious a priori case in which there can be no compellingly unique compromise is that in which I am offered a choice from an infinite set of possibilities, none of which has the greatest value (e.g., $1,000, $2,000, $3,000, . . .). But this, unfortunately, has not been a practical problem in my life.

Maximization is commonly treated as the basic meaning of rationality or, at least, as part of the meaning. In particular contexts we have no difficulty giving clear meaning to the notion of maximizing in individual choice over various alternatives. For example, given a choice between two outcomes, one of which I prefer to the other, I know what it means to maximize. If my choices or actions determine results only probabilistically, the notion of maximization is already in question. Most choice theorists seem to find the generalization to maximum expected utility an obvious extension of basic rationality, although some people do not find that move obvious or even right. The central problem of rationality in economics is that we cannot so readily or agreeably generalize our notion of maximization to many other contexts beyond the simplest context of, for example, choosing which amount of money to take from a list of mutually exclusive possibilities. Most especially, we cannot generalize it to cover contexts in which choices of different agents interact in producing joint, partially conflicting outcomes for the agents.

The theory of games was invented to model such choice problems. The difficulty in generalizing our notion of maximization to cover all games is that each agent is to maximize his or her own utility function over all the outcomes, but that different agents may have quite different utility functions over those outcomes. If you and I are maximizing, we are most likely maximizing over different functions. Although it is not always impossible to maximize over two functions at once, it is not possible to do so in general or to specify a general rule for doing so. For example, in a round of poker, you and I cannot both get our maximum payoffs of the whole pot. A trivial case in which genuine multiple maximization is possible is when our maximums are all in the same outcome even though our functions are not otherwise identical, as in certain coordination games. For example, when we are out driving, my welfare and yours are both highest when we follow the same strategy or rule of the road so that we do not have accidents.

Despite special cases such as these, however, it is still true that there is mathematically no solution to the general problem of multiple maximization. Vernacular claims that you should, for example, choose the vacation that would give you the most pleasure for the least money for the longest time are most likely to be nonsense. You most likely cannot maximize all three of these at once. For example, the most pleasure might well come at a very high price and might not last very long. Similarly, if there are three of us choosing a joint activity, we might be able to maximize for all three of us at once, but we very well might not. Hence, much of game theory, and of choice theory and economics more generally, is directed at finding compromises to multiple maximization that seem to be what one would deduce from the principle of individual maximization. In this sentence, *seem* is the difficult term, and its meaning is woefully ill defined.

There is no straightforward inference to multiple maximization from singular maximization, and game-theoretic solution theory is therefore, as should surprise no one who thinks about this problem, a morass. A mathematician would simply say, "Of course—there is no way to maximize over two or more independent functions at once." To trick up a solution to this problem for the general game would be as impossible as squaring the circle with nothing but Euclid's tools. As compelling as some compromises might be in certain contexts, they are still not as compelling as maximization over a single function that has a greatest value at some point or points. Game theory is an artful collection of such compromises. More generally, beyond basic rationality we need additional principles—perhaps many of them—to handle the complexities we face. Those who agree on the two principles of basic rationality need not agree on any additional principles, none of which has the compelling appeal of basic rationality.

The first success of game theory (before there was a game theory) was John von Neumann's saddle-point theorem for two-person constant-sum games such as two-person poker or chess. In such a game, the two players have inversely related utility functions over the outcomes. Clearly, it is impossible to maximize both functions at a single outcome. But because the game is constant sum, these two functions are not independent, so that there might be a plausible compromise to simultaneous maximization, maximization subject to a constraint. In the two-person constant sum game both players face the same constraint, defined by the inverse of each player's own utility function over the outcomes. For such games, von Neumann proposed the maximin strategy. If I follow the maximin strategy, I survey my possible strategy choices and the range of payoffs in each of them, and I choose that strategy in which my minimum payoff is higher than my minimum in any other strategy, or is at least as good as the minimum in any other strategy. This maximin strategy seems compelling to virtually every game theorist who has considered the problem.

One may say that this is a compelling compromise that seems consistent with what we would expect from maximizing players, given that maximization is mathematically impossible for both at once. But the description of that solution—maximin—is not a good prescription for a solution to the general case in which the functions over which we are simultaneously trying to maximize may be independent so that we do not face analogous constraints.

There are other contexts in which multiple maximization—that is, maximization over more than one function at once—seems to have compelling implications. First, in a pure coordination game, such as in the driving convention in which either we all drive on the left side or all on the right side, there can be a multiple maximand for all of us. Even for a game that is modally or approximately coordination, there may be a multiple maximand. Second, in a market of many sellers and many buyers, whose utility functions over all possible outcomes of trade cannot be simultaneously maximized, we may nevertheless expect a very restricted range of possible outcomes to result. Again, although the argument may be a bit convoluted, this result follows from what seems similarly to be a compelling compromise implicit in or consistent with the notion of individual maximization. All players in the market face the constraint that large numbers with similar interests typically imply the failure of collective action to collude on prices for sale or purchase, so that competition—between sellers and also between buyers—forces prices to a stable level.

ITERATED PRISONER'S DILEMMA

Few problems in game theory have generated as much discussion as the iterated prisoner's dilemma (the one-shot prisoner's dilemma is represented in game 1, in which payoffs could be taken as dollars), especially when it is iterated a fixed number of times, such as a hundred times. Merrill Flood and Melvin Dresher, the discoverers (or inventors?) of the prisoner's dilemma, actually first explored it in a game of exchange and in the many-play iterated form (Flood 1958; see further, Hardin 1982a, 16, 23–25). The game is represented in game 1 (fig 2.1). Fascination with this game comes from the peculiarity of its strategic structure. Each of the players would rather defect than cooperate no matter what the other does. But if they do, their payoffs are (0,0) when, by cooperating, they could have done better (1,1). What seems individually rational is jointly "irrational."

The label *prisoner's dilemma* comes from A. W. Tucker, who gave the story of two prisoners faced, in separate rooms, with offers to turn state's witness against his partner in crime.[2] The label is unfortunate in that it radically trivializes the game, which is also the payoff structure of ordinary exchange (Hardin 1982b). I once gave a talk to a philosophy department in which I said that a prisoner's dilemma game matrix represented simple exchange, with the natural implication that it was morally okay to play cooperatively, as in making an exchange. I was severely chastised by someone in the room who insisted that I had entirely misunderstood the problem, which was about prisoners who had done something WRONG. For them to cooperate in lying to the police would add a further wrong. The game was therefore a paradigm of immorality. The name of the game does not mislead everyone so perversely, but it does cover over what should be made far more evident: that its incentive or payoff struc-

		Column	
		Cooperate	Defect
Row	Cooperate	1,1	-1,2
	Defect	2,-1	0,0

Fig 2.1 Game 1: Prisoner's Dilemma

ture also represents exchange, a pervasive kind of social relation without which society would be a disaster.

Very early it was proposed that if it is rational to defect in a single-play prisoner's dilemma, by the argument above, then it is also rational to defect in every play in a fixed iteration of plays of the game. The argument, from so-called backward induction, is that it must be rational to defect on the last play because there are no longer any incentives from future plays to encourage one to cooperate on that play. But then that last play cannot provide incentives in prior plays, and both players must know this to be true, so that it must be rational to defect on the next to last play—and so on back to the first play. (The formal proof by induction is given in the appendix to chapter 2.)

There have been many practical and theoretical objections to that conclusion, and there have been many and varied proposals for seemingly more sensible resolutions. There seems to be a substantial consensus, which is not unanimous, in favor of the good sense of cooperating for at least many plays before finally defecting near the end of the run. None of these arguments claims that there is an alternative determinate strategy choice, merely that the backward induction leads to an implausible conclusion contrary to good sense. I will not claim there is some other "best" strategy, but merely that the demand for determinacy is not sensible, which means that there is no best strategy.

Many have noted that the players in a prisoner's dilemma that is iterated many times could do better than the mutual always-defect outcome. But this sounds like basic rationality: to choose more rather than less. Already Duncan Luce and Howard Raiffa supposed that rational players would cooperate for the first ninety or so plays of a one-hundred-play prisoner's dilemma (Luce and Raiffa 1957, 97–102; see also Radner 1980; Hardin 1982a, 138–54; Kreps et al. 1982; Sorenson 1988, 344–61). Unfortunately, it is not clear what it would mean to maximize in this context. Nor can anything like the Luce and

Raiffa solution be in equilibrium under a given equilibrium concept. Of course, the always defect strategy also does not maximize. We could say that a particular strategy would maximize only against some particular strategy followed by the other player. If that other player's strategy were determinate, then I could know how to maximize. If we constrain rational choice to yield only the always-defect strategy, then it follows that each can maximize with respect to that strategy only by playing it.

To deal with such problems as the apparent irrationality of always defecting in a finitely iterated prisoner's dilemma, game theorists have proposed many equilibrium concepts and other tricks to single out better results than the sometimes dismal equilibrium of always defecting (the best known of these is probably that of Kreps et al. 1982). The equilibrium concepts include proper, perfect, subgame perfect, sequential, and persistent equilibrium. These are not equivalent and some may fairly be called arcane. All of the debate here is over what counts as a good rational choice theory.

Let us start the play of our iterated game over. You and I are rational choosers. You come to the iterated prisoner's dilemma with the presumption that there is a determinate rational choice for you to follow. That choice is to defect on every play, as deduced from the backward induction argument. This is a *strategically determinate* strategy, because it follows from the logical arguments about how each of the players must reason in the iterated play. The actual world is not necessarily determinate—someone might even interrupt our play long before the ground rules said it would be terminated. But the logic of the reasoning to the always-defect strategy is determinate.

My task, if I disagree with your view that this strategy is determinate, is to shake your view of its determinacy. I can do that readily enough by simply violating its recommendation for how to play the game. I can cooperate rather than defect on the first play. When I do that, you must now decide how to respond. You can suppose I am simply too dumb to know what is the right choice, but that means the outcome of our play is no longer determinate. Now you can take advantage of my cooperativeness by cooperating in return in order to induce me to continue to cooperate. If that ploy works, you are much better off than you would have been if we both had followed your supposedly determinately correct strategy of always defecting.

Now you and I succeed in gaining substantially from mutual cooperation in this odd game. *But this is not the end of the analysis.* Note that you have benefited from the fact that I rejected the determinate strategy (or maybe was only ignorant of the arguments for it). You could as well have benefited by rejecting it yourself. But this just means that rejecting the always-defect strategy is better for you than following it. That is to say, in our ordinary sense of the term, *it is rational for you to reject that strategy.* That strategy was ostensibly justified because it is supposed to be rational. Note that here we have a reason to reject the always-defect strategy, but we do not have a reason for asserting that any other strategy is rational.

Indeed, in the present state of theory, we should hold open the possibility that someone will convince us of the superiority of another theory that we have not previously considered. Hence, when we begin playing our one-hundred-times iterated prisoner's dilemma, if I cooperate on the first or some early move, you should reconsider your theory. As Frank Hahn (1984, 59) suggests in another context, one should abandon one's theory when it is "sufficiently and systematically falsified." Let us see what follows from this advice. If you are, say, twice as modest as the average academic game theorist, you will likely reconsider the wisdom of continual defection once I have cooperated and thereby wrecked your expectations in our iterated prisoner's dilemma. Here we do not invoke the trembling hand, which might mistakenly choose the wrong strategy, or miscalculation, or any variant of what might be called error. Rather, we invoke a trembling intellect that, rightly, has reason to doubt its own theory In this case, by violating my own theory I can expect to improve my own long-term payoff. But that just means my theory is self-contradictory (Hardin 1982a, 149; for related but more complex views see Bicchieri 1988). If a theory recommends its own violation, it is not in equilibrium, as noted above. The theory not only trembles, it collapses.

Where does this leave us? Evidently, we are stuck with indeterminacy in game-theoretic solution theory and in rational choice theories more generally. Our theory cannot tell players in an iterated prisoner's dilemma fixed to run, say, one hundred plays that they should cooperate for most of the plays and then start defecting at the ninety-eighth play even if the other is still cooperating on the ninety-seventh play. It can only say that efforts at cooperation may be individually rational until far along, perhaps until nearly the final play of the series. If the series is short—say, two or three plays—the theory might commend defection all the way if it commends defection in the single-play game. And, of course, if the negative payoff for cooperating while the other defects is very large relative to the difference between the both-cooperate and the both-defect payoffs (say, it is $-1,000$ rather than -1 in matrix 1), it may not be rational to cooperate at all, because the potential losses from even a single cooperation with a defector would far outweigh any potential gains from many joint cooperations.

Although this argument has been in print for nearly twenty years, it has not found favor (Hardin 1982a, 145–50). Accepting the argument requires giving up on the effort to make the world of choice determinate and accepting strategic indeterminacy. Other cooperative solutions of the iterated prisoner's dilemma rely on presumptions that the world is somehow unstable, so that although the *reasoning* itself is still assumed to be determinate, and therefore correct, there is the possibility of error or a "trembling hand" that accidentally produces a cooperation that breaks the further application of the determinate reasoning.

That is, we salvage the disaster of determinate reasoning by bringing in an indeterminate real world, a plebeian variant of a deus ex machina, when all else fails. This is the wrong move. *The determinate reasoning is the problem, and it should be rejected.* Why have there been so many efforts to justify cooperation in a long iterated prisoner's dilemma? Because it is prima facie silly to follow the determinate strategy when there are such gains to be made as would follow from successful cooperation over most of the plays of the game. We know this very well in life, but we do not seem to know it in theory.

A standard, leaden response to this argument is that if you cooperate on the first play, I can exploit your naïveté and defect, thereby receiving a nice gain at your expense. If our potential run of plays is very long, say a hundred or a million, the gain will not be all that nice because it will be dwarfed by what I could have got by testing and matching your cooperativeness. But the response is even worse than leaden because it openly grants the indeterminacy at issue. Playing cooperatively is not a maximizing or determinate strategy, but neither is attempting to exploit a potentially cooperative player. It would be wrong to say that we can deduce the correctness (meaning determinacy) of the cooperative testing of the other player. We cannot because there is no determinate solution to this dual maximization problem of my wanting the best possible for myself while you want the best possible for yourself. It is logically impossible that we can both succeed in achieving our bests. To do merely well, rather than maximizing, we have to choose contingently in response to how the other chooses. There is no determinate resolution of the game, and every leaden response that some contingent strategy is better than another can be answered with the true claim that against that strategy there is another that is best for the other player.

The only strategy that does not have a better strategy as a response to it is the completely noncontingent strategy of always defecting. It is only dogma that says that is a good strategy. In any case, it is a strategy that defines away the social interaction as its device for achieving a fake determinacy. It also turns the play of the game into, at best, a contest in which you might beat me when the point of such an interaction is to do well. Indeed, a frequent claim about potential strategies for iterated prisoner's dilemma is that one strategy *beats* another. Strangely, the dogma is rejected by major game theorists, as already reported by Luce and Raiffa (1957, 100, 102) who, in their magisterial survey of game theory in the midfifties, "predict that most intelligent people" would not defect from the beginning and throughout a long series. One might also cite the manifold efforts of many game theorists over the decades to find reasons to argue for cooperation in the iterated play. It is mostly non–game theorists who hold to the dogma of continuous defection once they have heard the cute argument from backward induction.

As noted, a surprising number of recent equilibrium concepts in game theory seem to have been motivated at least partly by the compelling intuitive sense that the always-defect strategy in finitely iterated prisoner's dilemma is not rational. To suppose it is rational is to suppose that very good game theorists would play always-defect for hundreds, thousands, or more plays if only the trial is to terminate after a set number of plays. That is an absurd supposition. This is only an intuitive claim for cooperation, but it is a firmer intuition than any intuition that rational solution theory must be determinate or must produce standard equilibrium outcomes in ongoing contexts. It appears to be an intuition shared by many, perhaps most, contemporary game theorists, who seem to be motivated by the evident failure of the standard equilibrium argument of backward induction.

Perhaps the demand for determinacy comes from earlier simplifying assumptions of complete and perfect information. If we all have complete information about what all others are going to do, and they have complete information about us, the outcome of our interactive choices must be determinate, at least as from now. But again that means it must be an equilibrium. If it were not, at least one of us would have incentive to act in some way other than that in which complete and perfect information says he or she will act. One might suppose that this is paradoxical and therefore conclude that the assumption of complete information on future choices is an incoherent notion.

Whatever motivates that demand, however, requiring *determinacy in rational choice theory is less compelling than the urge to prefer more to less value in our interactions.* To require determinacy sets up the cute claim that it is rational to act irrationally in iterated prisoner's dilemma, because it is beneficial to act cooperatively despite the rational dictum always to defect. As Harsanyi (1977, 10) notes, for game theory we must go beyond the rationality postulates of individual decision theory, or we cannot resolve our problems. Iterated prisoner's dilemma seems to provide a major litmus test for the general applicability of various extensions of the notion of rationality. Determinacy fails that test.

DOMINANCE

In single-play prisoner's dilemma, there is a simple consideration that makes defection seem compelling: Defection dominates cooperation, which is the only other pure strategy. (It therefore also dominates every mixed strategy.) One of Row's strategies dominates another if the payoffs in the former are all at least as good as and sometimes better than the payoffs in the dominated strategy no matter what strategy Column chooses. Consider Row's strategies and consequent payoffs in the prisoner's dilemma, as presented in matrix 1 (fig. 2.2). If Column cooperates, Row is better off defecting; and if Column defects, Row is still better off defecting. Hence, defecting dominates cooperating in this game. That is to say, if there are no considerations outside this single play of

		Column	
		Cooperate	Defect
	Cooperate	1	-1
Row			
	Defect	2	0

Fig 2.2 Matrix 1: Prisoner's Dilemma, Row's payoffs only

the game, Row is better off defecting no matter what Column does. Defecting or, more generally, playing a dominating strategy sounds like a reasonable version of choosing more rather than less, and therefore of basic rationality.

In iterated prisoner's dilemma, always-defect does not dominate all other strategies. It may be said to chain-dominate them, as in the backward induction argument. For example, tit-for-tat all the way (call this T) is dominated by tit-for-tat with defection on the last play (call this $T - 1$). The latter is dominated by tit-for-tat with defection on the last two plays (call this $T - 2$), and so forth. But chain dominance is not a compelling principle for choice. It leaves open the possibility that, for example, $T - k$ is dominated by T. In pairwise choices over various strategies, always-defect might lose to many other strategies. In any case, there are many strategies it does not dominate. To force its selection by imposing determinacy or equilibrium conditions on final outcomes goes well beyond the primitive notion that it is rational to choose more rather than less value or to have transitive preferences.

One proposed principle for defending the rationality of the always-defect strategy is the sure thing or dominance principle, which sounds misleadingly like a transitivity requirement *over strategy choices, not over outcomes*. Strategy A dominates strategy B; we eliminate B. Now among the strategies in the newly reduced set, C is the strategy our theory selects. But this does not entail transitivity of dominance or even of strategy rankings. If B were still in the set, it might be chosen over C because it beats C for some strategy choices of other players and never does worse than C. Under our theory without the elimination of dominated strategies, we prefer C to A to B to C.

If A, B, and C were states of affairs or values, we would want our preferences over them to be transitive. Does it make sense to have intransitive preferences over *strategies*? It would be wrong to have intransitive preferences over strategies if the strategies determine outcomes directly—for example, if all other players' strategy choices are already known. But this is because under these

	Column		
		C1	C2
R1		1	3
Row			
R2		4	2

Fig 2.3 Matrix 2: Pure Conflict, Row's payoffs

conditions, intransitive rankings of strategies entail intransitive preferences over states of affairs.

More generally, however, it is odd even to speak of preferences over strategies. What we normally speak about is preferences over alternative states or over different values. Then we may rank strategies according to the payoffs we expect them to bring us. My choice of any strategy will bring me a return that is a function of what strategy you choose. To determine what I expect my return to be in an iterated interaction, I must estimate what you will likely do in response to my strategy choice. Then I may say, in the ordinary way, that I prefer the likely state of affairs that follows from my choosing one strategy to the likely state of affairs that follows from my choosing the always-defect strategy. In a many-times-iterated prisoner's dilemma with reasonably favorable ratios of the payoffs, one suspects that almost everyone would choose to play cooperatively to some extent to engender cooperation—unless they are blinded by perverse theory.

How does dominance stack up against maximin? Consider the ordinary pure conflict game, to which von Neumann's maximin strategy can be applied. Consider matrix 2 (fig. 2.3), which represents Row's payoffs in a pure conflict game (in this case, a zero-sum game, so that Row's payoffs are the negative of Column's payoffs). Note that Row does not have a dominant strategy choice but does have a maximin strategy. The maximin is strategy R2, in which the minimum payoff, 2, is greater than the minimum payoff, 1, in Row's only alternative strategy.

In this game, game theorists insist that the maximin strategy is the rational strategy for both players. If they both play their maximin strategies, Row's payoff is 2 (and Column's is the negative of this, − 2). If Column (irrationally) chooses C1 while Row plays maximin, Row's payoff is the best possible (4) and Column's is the worst possible (− 4). Note, however, that Row does not have a dominant strategy. If Column chooses C2, Row should choose R1; if

Column chooses *C1*, Row should choose *R2*. Hence, it is not true in general that there is a dominant strategy in games, although sometimes there is (even in some zero-sum games). *In particular, there is no dominant strategy in the one-hundred-play prisoner's dilemma if the iterated game is played as a single game with a strategy chosen at the outset for the whole sequence.*[3] In that game, every strategy is dominated by at least one other strategy.

Dominance is not a general principle of rational choice because it is incomplete, just as maximin is not a general principle because it is also incomplete. The argument for chain dominance in the iterated prisoner's dilemma depends on making the individual plays in the long iteration independent of any overall strategy, although it makes better rational sense (in the abstract) to treat a long fixed sequence as itself a single game, so that one can take contingent choices of the other into account in one's own choice of strategy.[4] Because two special principles for strategy choice—dominance and maximin—are incomplete and make no definitive recommendation in a fixed iteration prisoner's dilemma, these two additions to basic rationality are, along with basic rationality itself, indeterminate for this game. If this is true, then we should play the game as though the principle of rationality is indeterminate rather than imposing a false determinacy on it through the piecemeal argument from chain dominance. Chain dominance is a less compelling principle than is the indeterminate hope for a much better payoff than one can get under the dismal choice of permanent defection.

In any case, the argument from chain dominance is incoherent in that it depends on treating the long iteration as a series of individual games while also arguing from future plays as though they were part of the sequence taken as a single game. Because it disaggregates the game even while depending on its aggregate quality of being played for exactly *n* plays, backward induction in the iterated prisoner's dilemma is a false step. Chain dominance is an incoherent and irrational principle. Again, all the principles canvassed here—maximin, dominance, and choosing more rather than less—are indeterminate in social contexts of interactive choosing.

EQUILIBRIUM

Some of the results above—those that follow from literal maximization and those that follow from some compromise more or less deducible from it—are equilibriums in their particular games or interactions. For many contemporary economists that is not surprising, because they suppose equilibrium is inherently bound up in rationality. But the bonds go in only one direction. Equilibrium is defined in rational terms; rationality is not defined in terms of equilibrium. An equilibrium is an outcome from which no one would have incentive to deviate, by choosing a different strategy, even if it were possible to second-guess all the others in the interaction after knowing what choices they have made. It is not generally an outcome we would individually aim at.

A theory of equilibrium merely says that, if we get to an equilibrium state, then in some sense we will stay there. This conclusion supposes that we act independently. I stay with my strategy if it has put me in an equilibrium because, by definition of equilibrium, I would get a worse payoff if I changed my strategy while all others kept to theirs. It does not say that I have to choose a strategy that leads to or includes an equilibrium outcome. To make equilibrium in some sense a principle of individual rational *choice* would therefore be wrong.

That the equilibrium does not determine what is rational can be seen from the facts that (1) there can be multiple equilibriums with differing payoffs to various players, and (2) there can be equilibriums that are disastrous for all concerned and that are Pareto inferior to other possible outcomes. In both cases, it may be true that some subgroup has an interest in switching collectively out of the strategies that put them in the equilibrium. This is a principle of collective rationality, not individual rationality. In contexts such as the n-person prisoner's dilemma of the logic of collective action, we presume—often rightly as a matter of common empirical fact—that groups will not achieve collective rationality in this sense.

Again, equilibrium is defined in terms of individual rationality. If we are in equilibrium, then it would not be rational for any of us individually to choose a different strategy. Hahn has suggested an alternative notion of general economic equilibrium that makes the bonds go both ways in ongoing contexts, such as iterated games and normal life. We may restate his notion to fit game-theoretic choice problems: Agents in an interactive choice are in equilibrium if their choices generate messages that do not cause agents to change the theories they hold or the policies they pursue. (As noted above, Hahn supposes we should abandon a theory when it has been substantially falsified in experience.) This remark recalls Friedrich Hayek's (1948a, 34) observation "that the concept of equilibrium can be made definite and clear only in terms of assumptions concerning foresight." If many of us attempt to carry out our plans in interaction, then,

> in order that all these plans can be carried out, it is necessary for them to be based on the expectation of the same set of external events, since, if different people were to base their plans on conflicting expectations, no set of external events could make the execution of all these plans possible. . . . [Since] some of the data on which any one person will base his plans will be the expectation that other people will act in a particular way, it is essential for the compatibility of the different plans that the plans of the one contain exactly those actions which form the data for the plans of the other. (Hayek 1948a, 38)

Our plans will be compatible in relatively restricted circumstances, such as in interactions that are either pure or modal coordination. They will commonly not be compatible in contexts in which there is a substantial degree of conflict, although in two contexts of conflict they may be. These two contexts are the case of a market with many buyers and many sellers and the case of constant-sum two-person interactions, as discussed above. For many conflict situations, however, the standard notion of equilibrium makes little sense.

It is commonly claimed that the always-defect strategy in a fixed-iteration prisoner's dilemma is an equilibrium strategy in the sense that, if both players follow it, they find themselves in an equilibrium from which neither alone has incentive to move. The very idea of equilibrium falters here. Just as basic rationality loses its meaning in general strategic interaction, so equilibrium loses its meaning in an iterated prisoner's dilemma and many other contexts. To see why this is so, consider the form of the argument that defection is the equilibrium strategy in a one-shot prisoner's dilemma to the argument that the always-defect strategy leads to equilibrium in a long fixed-iteration prisoner's dilemma.

In the one-shot game, it is obvious that my strategy is not in equilibrium if I play cooperate, because I can do better for myself if I play defect. This is true no matter what strategy you choose, whether cooperate or defect.

Now consider a one-hundred-play iteration. Suppose you are Anatol Rapoport and I know that you always play tit-for-tat, meaning that you cooperate on the first play of the iteration and then you cooperate on each subsequent play if I cooperated on the prior play, and you defect if I defected on the prior play. We can say that this is your strategy for the fixed-iteration considered as a single game. Suppose I also have a strategy for the fixed iteration considered as a single game. Suppose we have been cooperating for, say, twenty plays. It is now true (as it is on each individual play of the iteration) that I will be better off on the twenty-first play if I defect. If I cooperate on the twenty-first play, my cumulative payoff (from game 1) is 21 and yours is 21. If I defect, my payoff is 22 and yours is 19 (the total is diminished). Of course, I will then be worse off overall because, under your tit-for-tat strategy, you will now defect on the next play. If I also defect on that play (the twenty-second), my payoff stays at 22. This is what my payoff would have been if I had not defected either time, but now it stays at that value so long as I continue to defect, even through the hundredth play. If I cooperate on that twenty-second play, my payoff falls to 21, but then it will grow thereafter if I continue to cooperate; but it will only be 99 instead of 100 if we both cooperate on every play thereafter.

It is false now to say that always defecting is an equilibrium strategy against you. Why? Because if I choose some strategy other than reciprocal cooperation with you, I will receive a worse—not better—payoff. When we treat the fixed-iteration game as a single game with each player choosing a single strategy for its play, there is no strategy that is rational or dominant in the way that there is such a strategy in the one-shot prisoner's dilemma. The only way to get a so-called dominant strategy is through some such argument as chain dominance. We could apply chain dominance to our entire lifetime and then we would defect on every opportunity for cooperation and we would be woefully poor. Of course, playing you as though you were Anatol Rapoport might be a mistake because at our first play you might defect and then ruefully smile at me and say, "I should have told you: I'm not Rapoport." My loss at that point might not be very great; if the payoffs in game 1 are in dollars, I would have lost $1.

Note that dominance does not automatically entail chain dominance, which is a new idea and is not conspicuously a compelling principle of rationality. But that means that the generalization of the notion of equilibrium is not conspicuously compelling either. If at complete equilibrium we are all dead, we should want to stave it off as long as possible. In sum, equilibrium is a coherent notion in one-shot choices, not in an iterated chain of interactions. Hayek (1948a, 35) goes even further to say that "the concept of equilibrium itself and the methods which we employ in pure analysis have a clear meaning only when confined to the analysis of the action of a single person and that we are really passing into a different sphere and silently introducing a new element of altogether different character when we apply it to the explanation of the interactions of a number of different individuals."

It is true that Rapoport's strategy of tit-for-tat with cooperation on the first round is different from an ordinary strategy in a single-shot game. But the iterated game is also different from a single-shot game in such a way that what counts as a strategy at all is inherently different. In particular, it is contingent. In the single-shot game, if we play simultaneously, there is no contingency. If, however, our strategies are contingent, then my choosing in this round in some way to influence your choice in a later round is a perfectly reasonable strategy. Indeed, it is the kind of strategy we use constantly in daily life, and for very good reason: It works to our benefit. I withhold from you today in order to get you to be more forthcoming tomorrow, or I yield to you now in order to get you to recognize the possibility of mutually beneficial cooperation with me. The range of contingent strategies is vast.

Dominance in the iterated prisoner's dilemma is commonly taken to be chain dominance from the last play of the sequence back through the chain to the first play. But when treated as a strategy for the overall iteration, dominance is cyclic. Every strategy is dominated by some other through individual choice to attempt contingently to change the other's choices. Against Rapoport, always-defect is dominated by reciprocal tit-for-tat and even by reciprocal tit-for-tat through the twentieth iteration with defection thereafter (and by many other strategies). There is no equilibrium for the whole sequence of one hundred iterations taken as a single game. There is at best equilibrium only for each play considered apart from the whole sequence. Chain dominance, incidentally, *is a new idea for iterated games only.* It does not arise in the original single-shot game. It is a principle that is brought in from the wings to resolve iterated play in a way that is determinate. It is not a clearly rational principle; it bears no relation to the simple principle of preferring more to less value. It is not part of basic rationality.

There are other differences here. In a single-shot prisoner's dilemma, mere communication does not affect assessments of interests in the game. I could promise to cooperate and it will still be my interest to defect, whether you cooperate or not. In iterated prisoner's dilemma, communication has the role it has in an ordinary coordination game. It helps us to coordinate on better joint strategies.

In the various solutions to the fixed-iteration prisoner's dilemma, playing irrationally, or with a trembling hand, or with a mistake is actually to be recommended to a single player. In these resolutions, if I get it wrong because I make a mistake, I am likely to do better (and you will also do better). But if I choose to get it "wrong," I am irrational. It is implausible to say that rationality is inferior to irrationality for a single actor. If we are sensible, we have to reject a putative principle of rationality that is worse than irrationality *by its own criteria* of yielding us more rather than less. The alternative, standard theoretical position is tantamount to saying that the supposedly rational-choice, equilibrium strategy is dominated by irrational or mistaken play. If so, then, again, it cannot be equilibrium. In conclusion, in the iterated prisoner's dilemma, determinacy and equilibrium hang together. And they die together.

CONTRACT BY CONVENTION

In a long iteration of the prisoner's dilemma, even if the exact payoff structure varies from play to play, players may develop a conventional resolution of the problem of cooperation. Because the prisoner's dilemma represents the payoff structure of ordinary exchange, which is often regulated by contract, we may call the cooperative resolution of an iterated prisoner's dilemma a contract by convention (see further Hardin 1982a, chaps. 10–14). It does not require the paraphernalia of a state, with its enforcement powers, to regulate such an interaction. All that is needed are adequate understanding on the part of the players and the incentives implicit in the gains to be made from successfully maintaining the play into the distant future.

I cooperate in the current play of the game because I want you to stay in the interaction with me and to cooperate with me in the potential future rounds of the game. If you do not benefit from our interaction because I fail to cooperate, you will de facto withdraw from the relationship merely by defecting on all future opportunities for exchange with me. My incentive is to keep you from withdrawing by making your gain from staying in the interaction far greater than what you would get from no interaction.

As it happens, we could write down countless possible patterns of strategy choice for our interaction. If cooperation is represented by *C* and defection by *D*, my strategy for the next five plays could be *CCCCC*, *CDCDC*, or any other pattern. Or, *in order to give you incentive to cooperate*, it could be some variant of tit-for-tat, so that I cooperate on the first play, and thereafter I cooperate if and only if you cooperated on the prior play. If we both play this strategy, we both sequentially choose *CCCCC*, although this represents the result of *the strategy choices* in each play rather than *the actual strategy that stands behind these choices*, which is the contingent strategy of cooperation in return for cooperation. (Recall that the always-defect strategy in an iterated prisoner's dilemma, which would result in the plays *DDD. . . D*, is not a contingent strategy but is supposedly an analytical deduction. It involves no concern with intelligently trying to influence the other player.)

Our lives must be a congeries of such contracts by convention. Our lives are mostly regulated by voluntary constraints and the infliction of sanctions no worse than mere withdrawal from interactions. We do not need the state or the law to get us through the day for most of these interactions. It may be necessary to have a state in the background to regulate many aspects of our lives, and if that state organizes our world in a sufficiently sanguine way, we can get by most days without much awareness of its role in our lives, which will primarily be filled with voluntary interactions with others.

Our diverse overlapping activities give us knowledge about each other that helps us to estimate, essentially from reputations, who is likely to be a worthy partner in an ongoing exchange. They also give us incentives both directly from anyone with whom we interact in this moment and indirectly from those with whom we might interact in other moments. And they give us enough activities of varied kinds that have the character of exchange relations that, de facto, our exchange relations are iterated.

Because conditions may change in any or all of these relationships, they are causally indeterminate. And they are rationally indeterminate in the way that iterated prisoner's dilemma is. Yet, it is a striking fact that we live our lives despite the massive indeterminacy and we manage extensive cooperations with others. *Pragmatically, we have great competence in dealing with indeterminacy.* If we are forced intellectually to recognize the indeterminacy, we might often find ourselves stymied. Some of us have such intolerance for ambiguity that we should be kept happily in the dark about just how indeterminate our incentive devices are. In many contexts, intolerance for ambiguity is intolerance for reality.

Our interactions with others in daily life are, of course, more or less open-ended most of the time rather than for a fixed number of plays. It is an appealing fact that plays in open-ended and long fixed-iteration interactions are not significantly different in their rational appeals. One of the oddities of the standard backward induction argument is that it implies that, if you and I face each other in a series of exactly one million plays of a prisoner's dilemma, we should defect at every play. Although there are differences of opinion on what happens if the play is to last approximately, rather than exactly, one million plays, many game theorists think that, for the approximate run, it is rational to cooperate rather than to defect up until the point at which you learn, if you ever do, that there now remain a fixed number of further plays. It is prima facie silly to suppose there could be such a devastating difference in these two interactions— approximately and exactly one million iterations of a prisoner's dilemma.

Some of those who insist on the backward induction argument also general-ize it to cover series in which there is definitely going to be a terminal play, even if the players do not know in advance which play that will be. In life, all our interactions will definitely terminate because we will terminate. In life, then, for these theorists, it would be rational to defect at all times with everyone in voluntary exchange interactions that do not have backing from the state or other outside incentives. Commonsense pragmatism is radically superior to this supposedly theoretical knowledge. And indeed, if these theorists acted by their theory, they would live isolated from society. Instead, they live among us and inconsistently taunt us with their theory.

Nuclear Arms Control

An example of the use of contract by convention in nuclear arms control might help clarify how it works (see further, Hardin 1982a, 209–11; 1984a; 1985). On 10 June 1963, President John Kennedy, in his "Strategy of Peace" speech, announced that the United States was unilaterally ending nuclear tests in the atmosphere and would resume them only if another nation did so. At that time, test ban negotiations had been underway for a long while with no clear prospect of success. Soviet Premier Nikita Khrushchev immediately reciprocated and went further, announcing that the Soviet Union would unilaterally cease pro-duction of strategic bombers. Numerous other unilateral steps were then taken, and in August the Limited Test Ban Treaty was signed.

In this relatively happy instance, contract by convention actually led to a treaty. But even if it had not, it might well have been effective in blocking atmospheric tests by the United States and the Soviet Union. Either the contract by convention or the treaty was possible, of course, only because both nations shared an interest in ending atmospheric tests, which were harming children in both nations by contaminating milk and other foodstuffs with radioactive cesium and other by-products of nuclear explosions. (Some of these by-prod-ucts made their way into children's growing teeth and bones.) It was easier, however, to initiate the cessation of tests by the informal device of contract by convention than by treaty. Indeed, contract by convention governed a very large part of all the successes in nuclear arms control between the two super-powers over nearly four decades. Even unratified treaties—such as the 1979 SALT II Treaty, the Threshold Test Ban Treaty of 1974, and the Peaceful Nuclear Explosions Treaty of 1976—were effective, because, after all, they were contracts by convention even though they were not yet ratified treaties. Moreover, after it formally lapsed in 1977, the SALT I Interim Agreement continued to be honored.

Arms control treaty negotiations were not merely glacially slow. They were often a stimulus to arms development. With no clear idea of its military value, American strategists, with strong support from Henry Kissinger, promoted the deployment of the cruise missile *as a useful bargaining chip* for the next round of arms control negotiations (Smith 1984). Zbigniew Brzezinski (1983, 307–8), President Jimmy Carter's national security adviser, later proposed that 572 Pershing and cruise missiles be placed in Europe. On his own account, he proposed such a large number in the expectation "that we would probably be asked by NATO to scale down or that we would have to engage eventually in some arms control bargaining with the Soviets." He wanted to be sure there were "numbers high enough to give the U.S. bargaining leverage with the Soviets."

Brzezinski later advised Carter to respond negatively to a 1979 offer by Leonid Brzezhnev to withdraw some troops from Eastern Europe if new Pershing missiles were not installed in Western Europe. Brzezinski (1983, 340–41, emphasis added) wrote, "While the Soviets *should* share 'a substantial common interest' with us, I felt that recent Soviet behavior demonstrated that such a common interest *did not yet* exist, and that we should make it clear to the Soviet leaders that their actions were not consistent with the notion of a stable and increasingly cooperative relationship." For several decades by then, the two nations already had shared a very substantial common interest in avoiding nuclear war. Seldom if ever have any two nations shared a graver or more urgent common interest. Khrushchev had understood the relationship far better. In his memoirs, speaking of Kennedy, he wrote, "He was, so to speak, both my partner and my adversary." That is exactly the nature of the prisoner's dilemma; it has strong elements of both partners' coordination and adversaries' conflict.

During the 1980s, I once gave a talk on this topic to the Lawyers' Alliance for Nuclear Arms Control (LANAC) in Chicago. During the discussion it became clear that about half the group were divorce lawyers, who are a small fraction of all lawyers. We all found that fact funny. One might have wished that contract lawyers were interested in the issue of arms control, because treaties sound like loosely enforceable contracts. But these lawyers perhaps showed the better insight. Arms control was played out in the most destructive way possible during the years after the limited successes of the 1960s. Contract lawyers knew this bore little relation to contract and were not interested. Divorce lawyers understood the syndrome and naturally found it fascinating.

National leadership on both the American and the Soviet sides seemed to be by colossal dullards, who were much happier accusing the other side of duplicity and evil intent than working out a way to live through that potentially awful era. Divorce negotiations are often similarly destructive, with the point, apparently, of making sure that the other gets as little as possible rather than making sure of one's own well-being (as in "winning" a long iteration of prisoner's dilemma rather than doing well in it). As some divorce lawyers evidently recommend, the best device for divorcers is to wait long enough that the acrimony subsides enough that they can view the process as one in which they strive to do well rather than using it to harm the other. The latter stance risked Armageddon for the nuclear standoff.

The actual lawyers who were involved in arms control negotiations might as well have been instructed by Brzezinski and Kissinger. They raised difficulties perhaps far more often than they managed any. In the face of actual experience, one lawyer insisted that "the *only* realistic and effective way we have of trying to control the arms race is through negotiating solid and legally binding international agreements with the Soviets" (Bilder 1985, 53, emphasis added). In this claim, "legally binding" means binding until abrogated. Because easy unilateral abrogation is built into treaty agreements, "legally binding" here is a vacuous phrase. Leaders who could come to understand the rationale of contract by convention, as evidently Kennedy and Khrushchev did, would have behaved better than most leaders, East and West, did in the days of massive nuclear deterrence. And they could have accomplished far more than all the treaties did. After getting reductions, they would have made it easy for lawyers then to write treaties that simply confirmed the new status quo. The instinct of the lawyers was to look for determinate resolutions when, in the iterated prisoner's dilemma of arms control, there was no determinacy to guide choices.

Mikhail Gorbachev recognized that the nuclear weapon system was only for deterrence and that if you are not a threat, you need not deter. He evidently believed that the United States was not a threat and that he could convince American leaders that the Soviet Union was not a threat by ending Soviet rule of central Europe and by destroying weapons. Kennedy, Khrushchev, and Gorbachev were relatively creative. The other leaders of the era were mostly dullards. George Bush failed even to grasp that Gorbachev's dramatic moves changed the system fundamentally. Neither the game nor the technology of nuclear deterrence is determinate. The key to resolving the conflict of those weapons therefore was to recognize the indeterminacy.

Against Determinacy

It is astonishing that, of all endeavors, game theory is so cluttered with concern for determinacy. The very idea of game theory—to map outcomes of interactive decisions by multiple players—is transparently, as a theory of choice, inherently indeterminate for the trivial mathematical reason that maximization of multiple functions is mathematically impossible in general. As already noted, if players' preference functions over outcomes of a game are independent, those functions cannot in general be maximized simultaneously. The beauty of countless little bits of interaction is that they do yield simultaneous maximands for two or more players. Descriptive game theory reveals by mere inspection which games are most likely to yield such beautiful results: coordination games and many messier games in which there is at least a predominant element of coordination. In such games, players' preference functions are not independent. Hence, there are three simple contexts in which determinacy makes sense: n-person pure (or at least modal) coordination, two-person constant-sum pure conflict, and a market of many sellers and many buyers.

The perversity of the prisoner's dilemma is that it includes a very important element of coordination (over the pair of outcomes defect-defect and cooperate-cooperate), but also an important element of conflict (over the pair defect-cooperate and cooperate-defect). Because of the substantial element of conflict in this case, there cannot be simultaneous maximization. Because of the coordination, there is a prospect of substantial individual gains, *but only if both gain.*

In sum, in the iterated prisoner's dilemma, determinacy would require players to defect at every play; but this is not a sensible strategy. Hence, we should conclude that determinacy is not a defining feature of rationality. If game theory and strategic interaction more generally are to be taken seriously in even moderately complex contexts, the demand for determinacy must go. The fixed-iteration prisoner's dilemma seems to entail an awful outcome only if it is assumed that we must want a determinate solution. Sometimes to know there is a solution helps us to find it. This problem, however, does not have a solution of the usual, expected kind and assuming that it does will not help us find it.

Suppose we have a determinate notion of rational choice. Then we can define an operator, R, which, when applied to any choice problem, will give us the rational choice. In the abstract, R must be agent neutral. If you and I are involved in a joint choice, we each apply R. But for me to choose well, I must take into account the way I should expect you to act. Hence, one of the inputs to my R will be your R, which is the same as mine except that it is over the different function of your payoffs (rather than the function of mine). Of course, you must also put my R into yours. Mine already includes yours, so that now your R must be applied to a function of your R. Therefore, we have a recursive function. Some recursive functions are perfectly well behaved, so perhaps this one is as well. Unfortunately, however, most writers on these problems have never actually proposed the content of such an operator, so we cannot be sure any of theirs will be well behaved. Harsanyi has proposed a content for R, but that content includes the stipulation that it must yield a determinate outcome despite the indeterminacy of our world.

If we do not have a rational operator, R, then our debates about what is rational in some context that does not meet the simple conditions of basic rationality are apt to be intuitionistic and ad hoc. This is virtually tantamount to saying that our understanding of the issues is indeterminate. We can conclude further that our understanding is indeterminate *because the problems are inherently indeterminate under basic rationality.* To understand these problems is to grasp that they are indeterminate. Tricking up solutions to them may make pragmatic sense in many contexts, but we should not go further and suppose that our tricks are fundamental to the conception of rationality. They are not.

A pragmatic rational choice operator would allow for the possibility that others misunderstand it or disagree with it so that, at least de facto, they are using a different operator. It would therefore not be determinate but must be contingent. It would therefore be far more nearly like the rationality of ordinary people than is any more pristine theory, such as some of the arcane solution theories in game theory. It would also generally accommodate seemingly open-ended relationships, such as that of the United States and the Soviet Union during the heyday of nuclear deterrence.

Concluding Remarks

In an iterated prisoner's dilemma, I might turn out to be as grievous a dullard as several American presidents and their advisers were when they faced arms control initiatives, and I might obstinately refuse to give up on always defecting no matter how many times you might try to induce me to do otherwise. It is a striking fact, however, that to be such a dullard in this case, one almost has to be a theorist, because an ordinary person would typically do better than this, as countless experiments have shown (Ledyard 1995). The theorist's obstinacy here is rather like the professional deformation of the lawyer who insists on extreme legalism in the effort to reduce dangerous armaments, and thereby locks the arms in place and induces expansion of arms systems in order to create bargaining chips. Neither the obstinate theorist nor the lawyer has the pragmatic sense to do well rather than to be rigorous and consistent while failing badly in making life go. Indeed, it is only a half-theorist who is so obstinate in an iterated prisoner's dilemma because, as noted above, many of the best game theorists insist that they would not play the game so destructively as never to cooperate.

Recall the seven responses to indeterminacy listed in chapter 1. Three of them have been elevated to theory by some writers. In particular, some variant of cardinal, interpersonally additive valuation has been proposed as a theory by Bentham, Harsanyi, and many others. The stipulation of determinacy in theory despite indeterminacy in the world to which the theory is applied is also proposed by some. The use of rules in, especially, moral theory is taken to be a profound theoretical stance by many moralists. Clearly, the acceptance of indeterminacy should also be taken as a fundamentally theoretical move. Three other responses are tricks that work pragmatically in some sense. Two responses—those of Hobbes and Coase—were intended as pragmatic devices, and they both work very well in the relevant contexts. Indeed, one might say, that is partly why they work so well, because Hobbes and Coase were specifically trying to resolve particular problems. Their devices have the appeal that the claims for them are relatively modest. There is no presumption that they are general solutions for collective choice. Claims for additive cardinal value theories and moralists' claims for moral rules are extremely immodest and, not least therefore, incredible.

Consider two seemingly contrary positions on rational choice theory. First, Robert Aumann (1985, 28–29) says that a game-theoretic "solution concept should be judged more by what it does than by what it is; more by its success in establishing relationships and providing insights into the workings of the social processes to which it is applied than by consideration of a priori plausibility based on its definition alone." Second, Reinhard Selten (1985, 81) replies that: "Descriptive theories need to be compared with reality, whereas normative theories cannot be tested empirically. The justification of normative theories of rationality must be sought in compelling intuitive arguments." Similarly, Richard Jeffrey (1983, 166) notes that the Bayesian theory of preference is ours—the theorists'—but not necessarily the agent's. The issue in this book is not with testing normative theories against reality, but rather with designing theories to fit what people should do in the face of reality.

The ideal conditions of determinate choice theory are not our conditions. Such a theory is, in this respect, not an analog of, say, the neurological theory of vision, which is also not the agent's theory. Rational choice theory is not descriptive, as the neurological theory is, but normative. This means, incidentally, that the normative theory of rational choice is very hard—indeed, it is essentially beyond all of us, including theorists. Much still remains to be resolved in the theory. Most of the solutions to the iterated prisoner's dilemma and Harsanyi's relatively general solution theory belong in the list of responses to indeterminacy in chapter 1. Except for the solution that acquiesces in the recognition of indeterminacy, most of the solutions to the iterated prisoner's dilemma are openly normative and, in this respect, *they resemble the moralists' response of stipulating rules for behavior, more than the theorists' response of attempting to find a way through the morass that makes pragmatic sense.*

Both rationality and equilibrium have clear meanings in simple contexts and then require increasingly elaborate, ad hoc, often intuitionistic additions in more complex contexts. While the original, simple meanings are compelling and virtually unassailable, the increasingly baroque variants that are addressed to complex social interactions are not very compelling and are often assailed. As quoted above, Hayek (1948a, 35) argues that "we are really passing into a different sphere and silently introducing a new element of altogether different character when we apply [equilibrium] to the explanation of the interactions of a number of different individuals." Clearly, we can say the same for rationality. Once we get past basic rationality, we are increasingly in a maze of complexity and ad hoc intrusions. These are merely aspects of the indeterminacy of our world. For even moderately complex games, including the fixed-iteration prisoner's dilemma, there is no strategy that is definitively rational.

Consider one last approach to the prisoner's dilemma for a long fixed iteration. One way to establish what is the savvy strategy to choose is to answer the question, If I were to establish a reputation for playing a particular strategy, what strategy would it be good to establish? In cooperative contexts of potential exchange, it would be beneficial to establish a reputation for being like Rapoport. It would not be good to establish a reputation for playing always-defect—that would lead to no offers of cooperation from anyone else. In ordinary life, as opposed to the conditions under which experimental games are commonly played, it is commonly possible to establish such a reputation. Again, this is not a determinate answer, because there is no determinate answer. It is at best savvy, not rational according to the principle of basic rationality. Such savviness is what we should actually hope for in social life.

Chapter Three

Mutual Advantage

I F WE CAN make nothing more than personal judgments, without comparisons or additions of welfare from one person to another, it would seem that we are reduced to merely individual rationality. In fact, however, we can make aggregate-level claims of mutual advantage, which, as argued in chapter 1, is the aggregate-level equivalent or implication of individual self-interest. In manifold minor contexts, there is little or no difficulty in seeing mutual advantage. For example, every voluntary exchange is an exercise in securing mutual advantage. Families can commonly join in doing things together that could not be done separately and that all would prefer to do in lieu of other things. The creation of orderly regulations for many activities that without coordination would be hamstrung is commonly to the mutual advantage of everyone affected, as in the ordinary rules of the road that make traffic flow smoothly or in the rules of law that govern manifold activities, such as contracting. Many ordinary customs work for mutual advantage by coordinating people. A large part of the activities that ordinary rules of morality are meant to govern are activities that, if well governed, commonly benefit all concerned. For example, telling the truth typically, although not always, serves the mutual advantage of the speaker and of the audience of the speaker.

Indeed, if they did not already prevail, many of the rules of ordinary morality and many of the norms and customs that govern our lives might well be deliberately devised by someone or some agency and promulgated through arguments that they are in our interest and should therefore be supported and followed, even to the point of sanctioning those who violate them, as though they were merely regulations for handling traffic among people. Many of those who keep promises and other agreements might not even require normative sanctions for violation because their interests are sufficiently at stake and they understand this fact well enough that interests alone motivate them. As Hume ([1739–40] 1978, bk. 3, pt. 2, sec. 5, p. 523) said, the first obligation to keep promises is interest. If we survey our daily lives and many of our larger social activities, we may be astonished at how much they involve interactions that serve mutual advantage. A strictly ordinal utilitarianism would commend all these activities as enhancing welfare.

In many of these cases, we might expect to convince you, as a party to the interaction, to act cooperatively because it is in your interest to do so, and this will typically be correct. One might therefore suppose that these are not meaning-fully conceived as aggregate issues. But such a conclusion is wrong; they are aggregate issues because they involve joint action or benefit or both, and they cannot work to our advantage without such jointness. You and I might both go for a walk this afternoon over the same terrain just for the pleasure of it. But we might not coordinate our activities, and we could then say there is nothing joint about the two activities. In this case, individual-level interests are the whole story. When I go for a walk with you because I want to spend my time with you, however, the activity is at the aggregate level and part of the benefit from it may be from the aggregation. Similarly, when I drive or walk on Fifth Avenue in Manhattan, where I have to coordinate movements with countless others, or when I buy something or participate in conversation in which truth matters, some aspect of the activity is inherently at an aggregate level.

Moreover, we are able to compare the value of one of these activities at the aggregate level to the value of some alternative. That comparison can be strictly ordinal. We do not need in some sense to add up the benefits and costs of the activity overall to decide on our collective preference for it over some alternative. We can make the comparison the way we compare sets in set the-ory. We lay the sets side by side and compare their members one to one. Each of us can compare the relative benefits to ourselves of one joint activity versus another, or even of a joint activity versus individual activity that is not joint.

Clearly, we cannot expect all such comparisons to come out in favor of particular joint activities. Sometimes I might prefer joint activity X to Y while you prefer Y to X. Yet we might both still prefer either X or Y to neither.[1] Now we might be inclined to weigh the strengths of our preferences, so that we do a cardinal comparison of my benefits to yours. As I will discuss in chapter 4, this will seem plausible if we are similar enough, know each other well enough, and so forth, actually to suppose we can make the relevant judgments agree-ably—as seems commonly to be true in, for example, very close and egalitarian relationships. Alternatively, we might find a way of packaging our joint activity now with an alternative activity at another time. I give you a rain check on doing Y in return for your doing X today. Packaging simply makes our mutual advantage cover a broader span of activities in order to make it more agreeable. But even if we cannot do either of these things, we can still agree that doing either X or Y is better than doing neither, and one of us might simply relent and do what the other prefers.

Social Order

Let us turn to the grandest of coordinations for the benefit of those coordinated: social order. The most compelling modern understanding of social order began with Thomas Hobbes. Hobbes's central argument for the creation or maintenance of a government was that government brings order where otherwise there would be destructive anarchy. In the order created by government, we can each confidently invest effort in our own property and secure our own greater welfare and we can engage in mutually beneficial cooperation. In the first instance government brings us safety from the depredations of others but, as Hobbes ([1651] 1968, chap. 29, p. 376 [175]) wrote, the point of government is not "a bare Preservation, but also all other Contentments of life, which every man by lawfull Industry, without danger, or hurt to the Commonwealth, shall acquire to himselfe."

Using our language, we may retrospectively say Hobbes's value theory was individualist and ordinalist. Hobbes may have had an antipathy to interpersonal comparisons rivaling that of Pareto 250 years later. Or perhaps the idea of interpersonal comparisons did not occur to him. He was concerned only with improvements to each and every person's existence, not with some additive notion of overall improvement. But his view was pertinently different from Pareto's in one very important sense. Hobbes was not statically concerned with optimizing welfare by reallocating among us through voluntary exchange what we already have. He was dynamically concerned with giving us the opportunity to produce more and thereby to increase our welfare.

Clearly, in moving from anarchy to government, we may have numerous possible governments to which to move. Some of these may be better for me, others may be better for you. Therefore, although we may agree in principle that all are better off with any one of these governments than with no government, we may not agree that one of them is better than all others. We therefore seem to face gross indeterminacy in the move from anarchy to government. Hobbes resolved this indeterminacy with a trick. He supposed we know too little about the effectiveness of various forms of government to be very confident of the superiority (for our own interest) of any one form over any other. In this invocation of skepticism about social-scientific knowledge, we escape the apparent conflict of interest over which form of government to choose. On the other hand, however, Hobbes supposed that the transition *from an extant government* to a new form of government would be too costly to justify any improvement it might bring—at least to the generation making the change. Why? The initial disorder would swamp benefits in the short run. Here, an unduly confident social-scientific claim secures commitment to an actual government.[2]

Hence, whether we are moving from no government to government or are already under a government, we face a simple coordination problem of getting to or staying at a universally preferred state. Our choice is a matter of mutual advantage, which, again, is the collective implication of self-interest (for a full account, see Hardin 1991).

A striking feature of Hobbes's view is that it is a relative assessment of whole states of affairs: Life under one form of government versus life under another or under no government at all. Hobbes thought that efforts at reform posed too great a risk of revolution and violent anarchy to be justified by their supposed benefits to us ([1651] 1968, chap. 30, p. 380 [177]). Most of the governmental decisions we actually face concern minor changes in what we have been doing. Many of these decisions would not even be called reforms, but even changes of a more far-reaching nature that might be called "reformist" seem to pose little or no risk of bloody revolution, as in the dramatic, relatively peaceful changes in 1989. As a social-scientific matter, therefore, we may disagree with Hobbes's blanket rejection of reforms. We may suppose that the reforms and lesser decisions of our quotidian political life are merely marginal changes in the gross form of government we have, and we do not risk full breakdown when we push for them.

Ex Ante Mutual Advantage

There is a class of stochastic policy choices that, ex ante, can be said to serve the interests of everyone, so that they are mutual advantage policies. An especially elegant instance of this class is widespread vaccination against a virulent disease such as smallpox, before it was eradicated, or polio, which has been eradicated in many nations and may soon be eradicated everywhere.[3] One might suppose that such a program is essentially to be justified by a cost-benefit analysis. Just because it serves mutual advantage, however, it requires no cost-benefit analysis other than the trivial one of justifying the expenditure on vaccination. Here the benefits are overwhelmingly larger than such costs and the benefits accrue to almost everyone, so that almost no one would have a preference not to fund the policy. Indeed, most Americans and Europeans must even reckon that the benefits *to themselves* of funding the campaign against polio in the Third World overwhelmingly outweigh the costs of that campaign, so that they might readily see it in their interest to pay the minor costs. Let us assume away these minor costs and focus rather on the stochastic incidence of burdens from the vaccination program in the days of domestic vaccination.

Our calculus for this program is easy to do precisely because it can be made de facto an individual-level choice over individual payoffs.[4] You want your daughter to be vaccinated, even though there is some risk that the vaccination itself will cause her to have polio. That risk is supposedly very much smaller than the risk that she will get polio if she is not vaccinated. Now we can adopt the policy of vaccinating, even of required vaccination for the receipt of certain public services, such as education in public schools, because it serves the interests of all in just the way it serves the interests of your daughter (and you). This is not an additive claim, but merely an ordinal claim. We can make this claim one by one across the population. Hence, our program is mutually advantageous, at least ex ante.

After our program of vaccination is carried out, however, some small number of our children will now have polio from the vaccination. Ex post, therefore, we could not say it served *their* interests to be vaccinated, because they might never have got polio without the vaccination. (It may be essentially impossible to prevent illness from vaccines in the case of diseases for which attenuated but still live vaccines are used, as in the case of the Sabin polio vaccine.) We take actions only ex ante, however, and not ex post, and what we must justify in adopting our policy is taking those actions. The expected costs to you of having your daughter contract polio from the vaccination are, again, far less than the expected costs to you of having her not be protected.

What makes the policy of vaccination a mutual-advantage policy is that we cannot know in advance who will be the losers from it. Government acts, therefore, as if from a principle of insufficient reason and supposes it cannot distinguish differences between citizens or the targets of its policy in advance. This example also has going for it that all are essentially alike in their interests, preferring a much lower chance of polio to a higher chance. If we can combine such a pattern of interests with the principle of insufficient reason to determine who will ex post pay heavy costs, government can act for mutual advantage. Superficially, one might think this conclusion strange: That increased capacity to judge the specific effects of policies in advance must make many policies more conflictive. Knowledge can hurt. But in fact, groups regularly mobilize to try to block political decisions that would make them losers.

Before leaving the case of vaccination, note the particularly grisly strategic structure of smallpox vaccination. Although smallpox has been eradicated among human populations everywhere, unfortunately it has not been eliminated as a possibility for humans. It cannot occur except in humans and there is no longer any source of smallpox in the wild. But there are stores of the deadly virus in two and possibly many other locations, where they might not be secure. Few people continue to be inoculated against the disease, because immunity wears off after some years, beginning about ten years after vaccination (which is done with cowpox virus, a less virulent cousin of smallpox). Few doctors might even be able recognize it today. *A potentially lethal side effect of eradicating the disease has been eradicating immunity to it.* Most Americans and Europeans, for example, are more than twenty years from their last vaccination or booster, and the young have never been vaccinated. Another side effect has been the elimination of stores of vaccine and facilities for manufacturing it (traditionally it was manufactured by scraping the insides of the hides of cattle infected with cowpox). A minor release of some of the stored virus could therefore set off the most devastating epidemic in world history, with perhaps hundreds of millions or even billions dying in the most gruesome way, in excruciating pain and in full awareness of their fate.[5] It is conceivable, therefore, that the successful eradication of the disease in living populations will lead to the worst possible result.

The only strategy that included the best possible result—the end of smallpox forever—included among its possible outcomes the worst possible result: the greatest harm humankind might ever experience. That harm was a risk of eradicating the disease. This is one of the worst imaginable instances of the nature of choice and action in a world of strategic interaction with others, which is the only kind of world in which one would wish to live. In its range of possibilities, the actual policy choice here is reminiscent of the policy of massive nuclear deterrence. If it worked, the world was at peace. If it failed, the world would be devastated. Both the eradication and the deterrence policies were inherently stochastic, with real prospects of the best and the worst outcomes. We were lucky with the deterrence choice. Our fate from smallpox eradication is yet to be determined. In both cases, stochastic indeterminacy and *the complexity of action when it is interaction* can have devastatingly harsh implications—or extremely good implications. Such facts confound much of simplistic philosophical action theory that implicitly runs an action into its consequence, as when I flip a switch to give light.

INSTITUTIONAL AND POLICY CHOICE

Now let us apply the conclusions from the example of vaccination at two stages: the policy-making stage and the preinstitutional stage of designing institutions that will make policies. If the two conditions in the idealized vaccination case are met, we can imagine similarly arguing ex ante for the creation of major institutions for the resolution of our problems, as in Hobbes's theory of how to deal with social order. In making his discussion very abstract, Hobbes essentially made it fit the two conditions of similarity of interests of all citizens and a principle of insufficient reason to distinguish their fates in advance of running the new government. This is one of the most brilliant and productive insights in the history of political thought, although its power has often not been properly appreciated.

Here I wish to focus on a less holistic version of Hobbes's problem, on fairly specific institutions of government rather than on government per se. Ex ante, we can give a mutual-advantage argument for creating an institution to handle some important range of issues. Consider some examples.

Common Law

It is a commonplace claim that among the most important values in the common law are the achievement of definitive resolutions of cases at hand, and the establishment of rules to guide future actions. We need resolutions of conflicts in order to let us go on with our lives. And we need legal rules that allow us to act in the confident expectation that our actions will stand against legal attack so that we may sensibly and confidently invest in our projects and our lives.

What the judge actually does in the common law when a case arises in a new context is to establish a rule to guide *future* actors while treating the present litigants *as though the rule had been in place when they acted*. This simultaneously accomplishes both the values of the common law. In criminal law, holding someone accountable ex post delicto to a new rule is objectionable. In civil law it is often virtually necessary. In the criminal law we do define new crimes and prescribe new punishments in response to new offenses, but we can do this without imposing punishments on those who gave us reason to revise the law. The miscreant merely goes without the new punishment. In the civil law, one or the other party to a complaint will be left in the lurch until a new rule is adopted and applied to their case.

Clearly, one of the litigants in a civil law case is likely to be a net loser from the decision in a case that establishes a new rule. Yet we may generally conclude that it is better to establish that rule than not to do so and that, whatever rule we establish, we must resolve the dispute at hand. If the parties to the litigation in the present case are similarly situated, so that both might be expected to gain more in the long run from one rule than from an alternative rule, we might easily suppose the resolution of the case to be mutually advantageous.[6] But commonly we would have to conclude that the actual decision makes one of the litigants a net loser in comparison to how that litigant would have fared under an alternative rule.

One might defend the common law case by case as being right on an interpersonal comparison of welfares rather than as serving mutual advantage. It is grounded, perhaps only implicitly, in the view that some parties' losses are outweighed by other parties' gains. Analogously with Hobbes's defense of having government, however, one might reasonably claim that having definitive resolutions of cases makes all better off than if there were no such resolutions. Hence, *the system of common or civil law serves mutual advantage ex ante*, although, again, one cannot claim that the details of a particular resolution make everyone better off. The normative defense of common law must be that it is meliorative, in the sense of ex ante mutually advantageous, rather than that it is morally right by independent criteria directly applied to individual cases.

Criminal Justice

For a second, more complicated example, consider a criminal justice system. Stochastically, we may know very well that the system will not work perfectly, as recent evidence of the innocence of many convicted people on death rows in the United States shows.[7] Of course, at an analytical or abstract level, many people have long known of this problem, although they may have had little

central flaws of the social contract argument. First, there was probably never an actual case of it. Second, even if we did all agree to empower one of us as sovereign, we would have no way to make our choice bind us to obey that sovereign, who would lack the enormous power of the kind of sovereign Hobbes thought we need for social order (Hobbes, *De Cive*, bk. 2, chap. 5, sec. 11, p. 90; see further Hardin 1999d, 146–48). Hobbes therefore supposed that all actual governments were established by force and usurpation or conquest. Although a—perhaps the—main point of most social contract theory has been to justify government and its power and to justify obedience to government, Hobbes understood very well that there is "scarce a Common-wealth in the world, whose beginnings can in conscience be justified," and he held that the sovereign's right is not justified by the rightness of his conquest but by the possession of the office that follows conquest (Hobbes [1615] 1968, pp. 722 [392], 721 [391]).

Perhaps the most influential contractarian philosopher who seemed actually to believe the social contract argument was Locke ([1690] 1988), whose importance essentially depends on the fact that he did not recognize, as Hobbes did, how empty the metaphor is. Locke did not grasp the essential impossibility of simply turning over power to a ruler or a government created de novo by contract. The contract tradition has since generally followed Locke rather than Hobbes. Indeed, even in writing on the views of Hobbes, scholars tend to read Locke into him and to focus on his ostensible contractarian argument for government, commonly making it a normative argument rather than a just-so story of how people might rationally behave if it were possible. Strangely, the contract literature has added virtually nothing to our understanding of the actual empowerment of a governor since Hobbes's recognition of the insuperability of that problem, so that Locke's oversight is now de rigueur part of the tradition.

Hobbes's just-so story gives an account of why we might see it as mutually advantageous to have a government with the power then to maintain order and to make policies that might not serve mutual advantage. He strictly divides the world into the ex ante choice of institutions and the ex post choice of policies by those institutions, although he does this just as well, as he insists, if our government comes via conquest rather than by contract. The later contract literature has tended to reduce contractarianism to an ideal theory—an ideal theory grounded merely in what we agreed to would not be very ideal and would, in any case, most likely be historically vacuous. Hence, contractarianism is now commonly grounded in what ideal people would have or should have agreed to.

The limit of this development to date is to suppose we can intuit what it would be "reasonable" to agree to (Scanlon 1999; Barry 1995). Oddly, at that point, the theory need no longer distinguish between the ex ante choice of institutions and the ex post choice of policies (see further Hardin 1998c). Both are subjected to the criterion of reasonableness, whatever its content might be.

Hence, at that point, Hobbes's brilliant insight is ignored, as it often has been since Locke. This is not a necessary conclusion of such theory, which could as well share with Rawls (see chapter 7), Bentham, and institutional utilitarians (see Hardin 1988, chaps. 3 and 4) the supposition that we must have two-stage theory (as discussed especially in chapter 8). Argument in defense of the current vogue of deliberative democracy similarly ignores Hobbes's insight. Indeed, claims for deliberation and the efforts spent on detailing how it would work are a way of hiding from the strategic indeterminacy that wrecks any hope for serious agreement beyond, with luck, a few general principles, institutions, and laws and maybe some happenstance policy choices. Because much of the argument for deliberative democracy focuses on policy choices, rather than on institutional choices, it is of very limited interest (see further Hardin 1998b).

POLICIES

Suppose we have a government whose creation makes sense as a mutual advantage move. Now it must govern by making and implementing policies. Few of its policies of any great import are likely to be as straightforwardly to the mutual advantage as is the elegant vaccination policy. Many of them might openly be made by trading off the interests of some for those of others. How do we justify these? In part the answer is that we already did justify them when we set up the government to act in certain ways. At that time, we might all have been subject to a relevant principle of insufficient reason. Indeed, we might even have wanted the government, once in place, to do cost-benefit analyses and to openly put burdens on some for the benefit of others, as is done with conscription and with the full panoply of welfare programs that serve some of the poor, most of the wealthy, most children, many corporations, all politicians, and so forth. That is the form of government we all might choose, even though we might seldom or almost never think any actual policy was to the mutual advantage (Buchanan and Tullock 1962; Brennan and Buchanan 1985).

This argument is partially analogous to that of James Buchanan and his coauthors in various works. They suppose that the standards of agreement for setting up a government or a constitutional order ought to be far higher than the standards for adopting a policy under that government. For example, they suppose it would be odd to use majority voting to establish that majority voting should be the principle by which we decide things. Unlike Buchanan and his colleagues, however, I am not making a normative argument on how we should go about doing such things. Rather, I merely note that we might readily agree on an institutional structure in advance as though from a principle of insufficient reason. Or, more generally, it might readily seem to be mutually advantageous to set up institutions in advance to do things that could not individually be justified as serving mutual advantage. For Buchanan and his coauthors, the ignorance of the constitutional generation about how the constitution will affect later interests is also an important consideration, but it plays its role primarily in their normative claims. In the discussion here, as in Hobbes, *its role is in defining mutual advantage or collective self-interest, with no further normative claim.*

Would it then be wrong to rail against a particular policy on the ground that it burdened some for the benefit of others? No. Not much in the way of staking out policy positions can be wrong in political debate. In such debate, one might even go so far as to say we would never have agreed to a government that would do such things—although most of us might well have agreed to just such a government. It seems inconceivable that a government that genuinely made society work relatively well could govern without making policies that fail the test of mutual advantage and that therefore reek of rational indeterminacy.

Hobbes could not even design the first stage of government to fit the mutual advantage of everyone—and he had only to compare his state to the grim conditions of civil war in his time. One wonders why an intelligent leader in power for more than a month or two in, say, Rwanda, would not ask some outside agency to come in and govern the nation. Presumably not the Belgian government and probably not even the French government would be acceptable to Rwandans. But even a large international corporation or a halfway competent government of any other large nation might do a better job than a local government, at least for the next generation.

Consider a complication of the pristine vaccination example discussed earlier. The live Sabin polio vaccine caused one case of polio per 560,000 first doses of the vaccine in the United States (Roberts 1988). But, as is typical of diseases that require human carriers as vectors, we might be able to reduce the total number of infections from vaccination by vaccinating only some large fraction of all children. The disease may not be capable of spreading if only some fraction of the population is vaccinated. (This fact was used in the eradication of smallpox, because everyone in the vicinity of a smallpox victim could be quarantined and vaccinated to stop the spread of the disease, which was exclusively by inhalation of the airborne virus from an infected person or perhaps from the deposit of exhaled, virus-laden aerosol on open sores or mucous membranes.)

Now we could say that, again ex ante, it would be mutually advantageous to all children to vaccinate only, say, 70 percent of them. Those who are vaccinated will be put at greater risk than those who are not. The actual choosing of which children to vaccinate is then not a matter of mutual advantage, even though selecting the percentage to vaccinate could be. (Of course, those children who do eventually contract polio do not ex post join in the mutual advantage of the vaccination program.)

Choosing which children to vaccinate has more the character of the choices made in a typical cost-benefit analysis, in which the costs to all are weighed against the benefits to all, although some may be net beneficiaries while others are net losers. In the United States, people have sued vaccine makers for their children's illnesses (see Sun 1985). The more sensible program would be to indemnify, from public funds, those who are harmed by publicly mandated programs. Then the ex ante burden would not be quite as far from the ex post burden as it traditionally has been. It is hard to imagine that many people would accept a promise of compensation in return for having their children vaccinated, however, and one might therefore expect the officials running the vaccination program not to publicize the fact that, say, only half of all children in a town need be vaccinated to protect all of them. It sounds perverse to suppose that keeping people ignorant might actually be mutually advantageous. But in this case, epistemological indeterminacy might enable government to act most beneficially. (This is, of course, not indeterminacy from strategic interaction or the presumptive principle of rational choice, but only of knowledge, especially popular knowledge.)

It is hard even to imagine a workable alternative to cost-benefit analysis in many contexts, such as the siting of roads, although there can be compensations to the net losers to, in legalese, make them whole. But for obvious reasons of the problem of strategic misrepresentation of preferences in order to gain advantage, the assessment of costs and benefits must typically be somewhat stylized rather than personalized. Hence, standard compensations may not satisfy all the losers. As in Hobbes's argument for government, having a system of imminent domain and stylized assessments of costs for public projects might be mutually advantageous in principle or ex ante. But its actual working in any particular instance is unlikely to be.

Concluding Remarks

Taking indeterminacy seriously as a ground assumption helps to resolve many issues. In chapter 2, I gave arguments for the resolution of the iterated prisoner's dilemma. Far more importantly, I think Hobbes grounded his theory of social order in an assumption of fundamental indeterminacy. That assumption yields his two-stage theory of government. First, we argue from mutual advantage for the value of government in resolving many detailed issues and making policies. Then, in the second stage, government uses various devices, including the presumption of interpersonal comparisons of welfare, to establish and effect policies. Metaphysical and normative objections we might have to, say, cost-benefit analysis considered on its own do not block our pragmatic preference for its use in actual practice in the two-stage theory, as noted in chapters 4 and 8.

I will take up some of these institutional issues more fully in chapter 8. For the moment, however, note that Hobbes resolved the greatest problem in political order by consciously and deliberately invoking the evident indeterminacy of the issues. No better resolution has been offered since Hobbes; indeed, most subsequent work on political order has been less masterful, because less insightful on this central, defining issue. This move defines the beginning of the modern understanding of politics by going as far as may be possible in grounding political order in individual interests rather than in an ad hoc claim of normative commitments.

In the next chapter, I will discuss a device that has been much less successfully employed to resolve indeterminacies: cardinal, interpersonal comparisons of welfare. This device borders on the purely normative despite its grounding in welfare as essentially interest. Then, in chapter 5, I will discuss a resolution of marginal problems in the context of an ongoing legal and political order, a resolution that simply accepts indeterminacy in interpersonal comparisons and nevertheless allows for mutually advantageous outcomes. Chapters 6 and 7 will canvass much less successful efforts to deal with indeterminacy, specifically in normative contexts: through moral rules and through a theory of distributive justice.

Chapter Four

The Greatest Sum

THE PROBLEM WITH ordinal welfare is that it often leaves us with indeterminacy. Indeed, in a large and diverse society, it would leave public policy almost entirely indeterminate. Only in a pristine case, such as a vaccination program without complications, can we expect to devise a policy that serves to the mutual advantage of virtually all. Vaccination against tetanus, for example, essentially benefits only the person vaccinated, while everyone not vaccinated remains at risk. A program to reduce the cost of such vaccination could therefore be mutually advantageous to all. If we had cardinal, interpersonally comparable values of some kind, we could determine which of two policies to adopt by simply checking the sums of utilities or other values to find which policy produces the better state of affairs. During the nineteenth century, economists and utilitarians typically assumed such cardinal, aggregative utility. This seemed to be an advance over earlier visions, such as that of Hobbes, because it allowed easy calculation, at least in principle.

Often the assumption of aggregative utility was coupled with the assumption that utility is objective, that it is a fixed measure of the goodness of an object. Developments in price theory in the latter half of the nineteenth century destroyed the view that utility is objective, external to the enjoying subject. For instance, the notion of the declining marginal utility of the consumption of any particular good implies that the utility is somehow that of the subject, not of the object (Stigler 1982). But once utility was seen as subjective, it seemed obviously individualist and not aggregative. Eventually, it seemed even that it need not be cardinal for the individual, but merely ordinal. Hence, even though I might be able to tell you very well how I rank various alternative states of affairs, it might seem unclear what it would mean for me to give cardinal, additive weights to those states—because they would be mutually exclusive and could not be added together.

Jeremy Bentham attempted to resolve the problem of indeterminacy in *evaluations of social states* by comparing states of affairs according to the sum of utility in each state. He supposed that each individual's utility could be measured cardinally and that the utilities of various people could be added. In rendering states of affairs into their cardinal, numerical utility value, we de facto create a set of numbers for comparison. If there is a finite set of states of affairs under comparison, there is a greatest element or a set of equally greatest elements. There might still be a trivial indeterminacy in the ranking of possible outcomes because two or more outcomes might have the same aggregate utility, but this is not a serious problem for the ranking of social states and it is not a matter of incompleteness as in the more general problem of indeterminacy of rankings based exclusively on ordinal principles of mutual advantage (as discussed in chapter 3).

In the event that there are multiple outcomes with the same maximal value, Bentham's cardinal device only helps us determine what is the best overall outcome. It does not necessarily tell *individuals* how they should choose or act. First, note that Bentham's solution could violate the assumption of mutual advantage because, for example, my utility could be greater in the status quo state of affairs than in the state of affairs to which it is proposed we move, and yet the latter might be ranked higher in aggregate utility. *Cardinalization of welfare therefore cannot resolve the problem of strategic interaction, which is the individual-level problem of indeterminacy of rational choice.*

Suppose, however, that we are all utilitarians who are primarily interested in the greatest sum of utility and only secondarily in our own personal outcomes. Would Bentham's move permit us all to make determinate choices as defined by the outcome that has the greatest sum of utility? Not necessarily, because there might be many patterns of individual choices that would produce the same overall sum of utilities. In some of these you would be better off, in others I would be. To give us a final outcome, there would have to be some device, not itself a utilitarian calculation, that would assign each of us our strategy choices. It could be a randomizing device or a capricious decision by government. Hence the criterion of utility, even interpersonally comparable and additive cardinal utility, would not be determinate.

Bentham's supposition that utility can be cardinally added across individuals is the main aberration in the line of development of ordinal thought from Hobbes to contemporary writers such as Ronald Coase. Something like Benthamite cardinal utility *for the individual* still has some appeal in some contexts, such as risky decisions (see Arrow 1973, 250, 256). And interpersonal comparison of utility has great appeal in some contexts. For example, interpersonal comparison is almost universally assumed by economists and social scientists who make policy recommendations, especially in cost-benefit analyses, and it is smuggled into standard treatments in law and economics. Cost-benefit analysis obviously assumes interpersonal comparison in adding everyone's benefits and subtracting everyone's costs to evaluate a policy. Richard Posner's wealth maximization principle for legal adjudication, discussed below, makes a similar assumption. But the rigid notion of accurately, interpersonally additive utility plays its intellectual role for us now chiefly in helping to clarify what is of concern and by showing ways not to go. Still, because rough interpersonal comparison is both useful and compelling in certain contexts, we might welcome a variant of the Benthamite value theory that could combine ordinalism with rough interpersonal comparisons.

As an aside, recall the standard Benthamite formula that we should strive for the greatest sum of welfare to the greatest number of people. This requires maximization over two surely independent functions and is therefore entirely incoherent and meaningless. This transparent fact will not stop people from citing the formula. But it is not a credible part of utilitarian theory.[1] This is, however, not at issue in the present discussion. Indeed, Bentham more commonly spoke only of the greatest happiness principle.

A further objection to Benthamite utility is that it requires a fixed point, a zero-utility level. Ordinalists reject this possibility as meaningless. They might go further and agree with many writers who assert the psychological point that we have no innate standard of goodness or value. For example, in one of the earliest explicit statements of the ordinal view of value, Hume ([1793–40] 1978, bk. 3, pt. 3, sec. 2, p. 593) supposes we judge value only by comparison, not by intrinsic worth or value.[2] His claim might be merely a psychological claim, but it seems likely to be grounded in the supposition that we could not make sense of intrinsic worth, but only of comparative rankings. It might seem to follow that we must be marginalists, that we cannot judge whole states of affairs. But this does not follow because we can make the kind of judgment Hobbes makes—order under government is better than violent chaos for virtually all—as a strictly comparative judgment. Thus, Hobbes and the other ordinalists do not require us to establish a zero point or a metric for how good any state of affairs is or would be. Indeed, for any marginal or holistic claim of mutual advantage, we could do a set-theoretic comparison of each individual in one state to the same individual in the other state.

Bentham's was not the only cardinal, interpersonally comparable value theory. Two others that would greatly simplify our accounts of the world, if they worked, are the labor theory of value and the theory of wealth maximization. These are both, in a sense, resource theories, so that they might not be expected to suffer from the subjective complexities of cardinal utility theory. In fact, however, the labor theory fails just because it is finally unable to accommodate to the subjective utility theory, because it is finally about satisfying wants through the value of objects. The wealth maximization theory does not have this liability. If either of these were a credible theory, then, as with Benthamite cardinally additive and interpersonally comparable utility, we would be able to resolve apparent indeterminacies. There is one further claim for cardinal utility that might be mentioned: John von Neumann's cardinalization of individual utility (see the appendix to chapter 4). Because it does not support interpersonal comparison, this cardinalization does not resolve the problems of indeterminacy that other cardinal theories would resolve if they were credible, and I will not discuss it here.

SUBJECTIVE BENTHAMITE UTILITY

In an exchange system, you and I might trade various things in order to enhance our own welfare. I yield things to you that I value less than I value what you yield to me in return. The end result is that we have increased the welfare of both of us. Therefore, logically, we have increased overall welfare, if there is any sense in this term. We have served mutual advantage with our exchanges. Note now that if value is inherent in objects, as Bentham sometimes assumed and as the labor theory of value implies, exchange makes little sense because either each of us is indifferent to whether we have our own or the other's good, or one of us would oppose the exchange.

Now suppose that we have Benthamite cardinal values and that these are not grounded in the intrinsic value of objects (as Bentham sometimes supposed they are), so that they are subjective. I have my holdings and you have yours. The way to maximize overall value is not for us to make exchanges that are mutually advantageous. Rather, we must simply allocate each of our holdings to the one of us who values it more. We have then increased overall (cardinally additive) welfare but we need not have served mutual advantage, because one of us might now be worse off than before the transfers.

How do the two systems—ordinary exchange versus Benthamite allocation with subjective evaluations of goods but cardinal utilities—compare? Any re-allocation that would follow from ordinary exchange between us would also be utility increasing in the Benthamite calculus, although it might fall far short of maximizing the sum of utility for the two of us. To put this somewhat differently, every voluntary exchange is utility increasing whether in cardinal or in ordinal utility. A Benthamite faced with a world in which it is hard to assess cardinal utilities might settle for the compromise world of mutual advantage, or merely ordinal increases. But in a world in which the Benthamite calculus could be carried out, doing so could massively violate the principle of mutual advantage in exchange. In our actual world, any would-be Benthamite, faced with deep difficulties in making and summing cardinal measures, should often compromise and accept the principle of mutual advantage.

There are two quite different problems with the Benthamite theory. The first of these is with interpersonal comparisons; the second is with the cardinal-value theory itself. Both have been the subject of thousands of pages of commentary, and we need not linger long over them. Indeed, I will say little about the problem of interpersonal comparisons here, although it will come up in other contexts.

The problem with interpersonal comparison is that no one has given a credible account of how it could work, so that many critics, such as Pareto and most contemporary economists, dismiss it as idle metaphysics. The problems with this dismissal are that many people are confident of at least some of their interpersonal comparisons and that almost everyone resorts to interpersonal comparisons in certain contexts. Many people think they can meaningfully compare the pleasures of their children and have no hesitation in deciding that the benefit or joy to one child from a particular activity outweighs the joy to another from some alternative activity. This judgment, however, is made easier or less objectionable by considerations of fairness. After yielding to the first child's greater joy on one occasion, the parents might choose the alternative activity on the next occasion.

An even greater pragmatic objection to dismissing interpersonal comparison is that it seems to be the only plausible way to handle many public policy issues. This might seem like a variant of the device of Coase, to be discussed in the next chapter. Under the Coase theorem, we can look at the money returns from two productive activities to decide how to assign resources to them. We assign the resources in the way that produces the greatest aggregate profit. But in the Coase system, this profit is then split between the two or more owners of the resources in a way that yields both of them more income than they could have got from employing those resources in their own mode of production.

The actual argument for cost-benefit analysis cannot be this quasi-Coasean argument, because cost-benefit analysis commonly or even typically entails losses to some and gains to others. It also typically entails substantial overhead, which might count for most people as a loss (but not to those whose living is made on that overhead). As argued below, some policies can be defended ex ante as though, from a principle of insufficient reason, we cannot know who will gain and who will lose, while on average all will gain. Hence, all gain in expected benefits ex ante, although not in actual benefits ex post. Here, the claim often has to be that the gains and losses are in welfare, and not in re- sources, which do not increase. Those who make or defend welfare programs must often wish they had a Benthamite utility meter.

Turn now to the problems with the cardinal theory of value, even when this is applied to value for a single person so that there are no issues of interpersonal comparison (see further Hardin 1987 and 1998b). We must, or course, be able to construct individual value if we are going to add values across persons. The chief problems with the theory are that it does not fit the way we behave with respect to various consumptions and that the way we behave makes far greater sense than the theory. There are two issues. First, if I consume one very good, full dinner tonight, I might happily pay market price for it. But I am very unlikely to want to consume a second at the same price and perhaps not even for free. Two dinners tonight would be, in this case, substitutes for each other, and I want only one enough to value it highly. Second, I might value some combination of consumptions far more than the sum of the values of the con- sumptions taken separately (as, for example, on separate occasions). Here, the two consumptions are complements.

Because of these two features, it is clear that subjective utility cannot simply map any supposed values intrinsic to objects. But it also cannot be simply an additive function of the subjective values of our consumptions. If our consumptions can be substitutable and complementary, then our valuations of them are not like a monetary measure. They are not cardinal. If my utility is to have cardinal values, I can define utility only for total states of affairs—taking into account substitutabilities and complementarities of all the items in my state of affairs—rather than for pieces of such states (Hardin 1987). But if I must evaluate whole states of affairs, there may be little point in assigning cardinal values to them. For many purposes it will be sufficient to determine a rank order for alternative whole states of affairs, as is supposed in the Arrow ([1951] 1963) theorem.

Labor Theory of Value

According to the labor theory of value, the value of an object is a function of the labor time that goes into its production. We can add the labor time from various contributors, but we can also add values inherent in various objects to obtain a total value, as in a gross domestic product measure, only that it would be tallied in labor time rather than in market values. Hence, the labor value is cardinal. It is also interpersonally comparative, indeed in two ways. First, if an object has a value, it has that same value to everyone. This conclusion is specious on its face. Second, the value added by an hour of my labor is equal to the value added by an hour of your labor. Those who happily pay exorbitant prices for a master chef's food must smile at this thought. These two objections amount to a criticism of the labor theory from the perspective of the standard subjective utility theory. Let us consider these two aspects of the labor theory of value in turn.

If the value of the object I hold is analytically or definitionally (rather than causally) determined by the labor time that has gone into it, then it would be odd to suppose that that value depends on who consumes the object. The labor value is now intrinsic in the object; hence, the object should be equally valuable to everyone. This implication should stop anyone from pursuing the theory further, except perhaps to find a way around this problem. As noted, Bentham did not get this problem clear in his own effort to establish a value theory. He vacillated between a subjective value theory in which value is, in a sense, in the consumer and an intrinsic value theory in which utility is in the objects consumed. Indeed, his use of the word *utility*—usefulness—belies his tendency to think of value as intrinsic to objects (Bentham [1789] 1970, chap. 1, sec. 3, p. 12). The perversity of this view is that it implies that you with your gourmet palate could not value an exquisite dinner a lot more than I with my wooden tongue do.

Price theory allows us to have even wildly different values for various objects. Hence, if I place a very high value on something, I would be willing to pay a lot for it. But others might be willing to pay much less. In the end, the actual price will be somewhere near the marginal cost of production. At that price, the object might be a bargain to me but very expensive to you. If the price goes below that value, the object will cease to be produced. If it goes much above that value, new producers will enter the market and compete for the excess profits, as Southwest Airlines does. On some routes that are served by Southwest, other airlines reduce their fares and some might cut back their service.

Obviously the object that I consume today might be made tomorrow with a technology that reduces the labor time for its production. That might or might not bring its price down. Computer prices have fallen dramatically over the entire history of their production. The machine at which I write this book fits in my briefcase, but it is more powerful and faster than machines that occupied large rooms when I was younger (and I am not *terribly* old). A decade or two ago, many people would have paid enormous sums for a computer as good as the one I use. Today, they need not spend much—they can use the excess to buy Rolls Royces and castles in Spain.

Now turn to the second way in which labor value is interpersonally comparable. My labor time is supposed to be equal in value to yours. Anyone who has enjoyed a wonderful meal at Arun's, Charlie Trotter's, Spago, or any other great restaurant would be startled to hear that the labor inputs of people are interchangeable. If they were interchangeable, why would anyone pay those prices when they could eat far more cheaply in restaurants not run by Arun Sampanthavivat, Charlie Trotter, or Wolfgang Puck?

Presumably, we could, with subtle effort, work through both these implausible ways in which labor value is interpersonally comparable to produce a complicated account that corrects for possible differences in labor quality and in demand. We then might have a theory that rivaled early models of the solar system in its complexity. But we would not have greater understanding of value. And we would not have helped to resolve the indeterminacies at the collective level that a genuinely cardinal, interpersonally comparable value theory would allow us to resolve.

The labor theory of value runs against the effort in many firms, especially earlier, to pay so-called piece rates. Rather than being paid by the hour, you are paid for how much you produce, so that two people working side by side might be paid quite different sums. Strangely, Soviet economies often used piece rates even while preaching Marxian exploitation of workers whose labor time supposedly determined the value of what they produced. Even the Soviet theorists of the labor theory knew better. One wonders what value they would have placed on their own work.

Wealth Maximization

Posner (1992, 12–16) has proposed wealth maximization as an alternative normative principle, at least for how the common law should decide certain cases that have allocational implications. Where rights are not clear, for example, we allocate a right to the use of a particular property to the producer who can produce greatest net wealth from its use. But we do this from the law, not only through bargains struck by the titular owner and a hopeful producer. We do so because we can thereby achieve the greatest productivity, *even in the face of transaction costs that might block bargaining*. In a sense, then, wealth maximization is a variant of Coasean efficiency (see chapter 5). But it is a variant with a Benthamite kick. It would be wrong to claim that greater aggregate wealth corresponds to greater aggregate welfare, but Posner does claim that greater aggregate wealth is a good thing in its own right (Posner 1981, 65–78, 108; see also Stigler 1978).

Wealth maximization without compensation is a genuinely cardinal concept that requires *interpersonal comparisons* of something—namely, money wealth. My wealth of $1,000 plus your wealth of $10,000 sums to a total wealth of $11,000. If instead I have $3,000 and you have $6,000, our total is only $9,000, which, under the criterion of wealth maximization, is inferior—even though I or a fairness theorist might think it better. Because one of us gains while the other loses in switching from one of these allocations to the other, the wealth test violates the principle of mutual advantage and is therefore not ordinally utilitarian.

Ordinary wealth is commonly seen as a resource rather than a good in its own right. It is good instrumentally because it is a means to various ends, such as welfare. The ordinalists' criticisms of cardinal utility would not apply to wealth maximization if wealth were merely resources, because resources are not a subjective value. Resource maximization is similar to basic rationality in that to have more resources is always better than to have less. This fact makes a criterion of resource maximization a great simplification of the limited range of problems to which Posner's wealth maximization is to apply. Moreover, wealth might be enough like money to be a credible cardinal measure. One might object that it does not map welfare or that it violates fairness, although these complaints are not clearly correct in ex ante judgments.

Unfortunately for the hope of such simplification, however, Posner (1981, 92) includes in wealth all past consumptions and even one's consumer surplus. Why? Resources are problematic because they are typically surrendered in return for consumptions. A welfarist counts consumptions as increments to welfare and resources as potential contributions to welfare, so that welfare subsumes resources. A resourcist who omitted consumptions from an accounting would count only unspent resources. In such an accounting, the painfully risk-averse miser who spent as little as possible would have greater resources than the more typical person of a similar income who led a life of fulfilling consumptions.

Including in wealth all past consumptions means that wealth becomes as complicated as cardinal utility theory. We might include consumptions merely according to their price, but this would mean that someone who wasted money retained as much wealth as our miser or someone who spent resources for a full life of wonderful consumptions. The initial simplification that moving to a principle of wealth maximization seems to offer is lost if we must bring past consumptions into it.

Incidentally, Posner's theory is relatively holistic in the sense that it is a full value theory, although he devised it to apply at the margin in court cases, just as Coase's Theorem does (see chapter 5). It falters as a full value theory only because we could not give an abstract weighting to various resources before we have a going economy in which to value them causally by what they can do for us.

Mutual Advantage and Interpersonal Comparisons

For anyone who wants determinacy, mutual advantage has the drawback that it is often incomplete, so that it often leaves us with indeterminacy. This problem is worse if there are many of us and we are diverse in various ways, in which case the set of possible mutual advantage resolutions may be severely constrained or even empty. But this problem is actually a recommendation for the use of mutual advantage, because in this respect mutual advantage mirrors the indeterminacy with which we have to deal in social choice. One way we can often reach mutual advantage judgments is by making them ex ante. This way we can assign expected changes in welfare to those affected by the judgments. Even after we expand the notion in this way, however, it will often still yield incomplete comparisons.

As argued in chapter 1, mutual advantage is the collective implication of self-interest because a mutual-advantage outcome serves the interest of each and every one of us in a collective choice. And, as argued in chapter 3, we may actually secure a mutually advantageous policy regime that does not itself use the criterion of mutual advantage to decide on policies. Suppose we design an institution for accomplishing various goals that we could not accomplish without the institution and we wish to assign the institution methods for aggregating our interests. What methods would we choose? Would we choose mutual advantage? Plausibly not, for the reason that it would be indeterminate in too many contexts in which we might need definitive policies. We might, rather, choose to have our institution use cost-benefit analysis (CBA) or other comparative, non-mutual-advantage devices in some contexts. For example, we might use CBA in such standard contexts as those in which, in fact, it is commonly used, as in siting of roads, building of dams, and so forth.

In using CBA, our institution would assign values—costs and benefits—to each of us, or to typical citizens, and would then sum these. We might all agree that this exercise is metaphysically perverse. And yet we might also agree that *we are all better off if we have our institution and if it uses CBA* in order to reach determinate resolutions of policy issues. CBA has the quality of the common law in that it resolves matters so that we may proceed with our lives. Having determinate outcomes is often a good thing, even when we do not have a determinate theory for how to get them. Hence, from a mutual advantage argument, we might recur to essentially interpersonally comparable cardinal values, not as a metaphysical claim about what is at issue, but as a pragmatic device for resolving our problems. Insofar as it would work to resolve these problems, it would be mutually advantageous to use it. This is not Coase's device, discussed in chapter 5, but it has a similar two-stage quality, with noncomparable ordinal assessments in the first stage and cardinal assessments in the second stage.

This is in fact a very powerful claim that almost no one could entirely reject, at least in principle. Virtually everyone now alive would be ex ante worse off without major institutions. Therefore, ex ante, having institutions is ordinally utilitarian. This does not determine which institutions to have but it leaves us a free hand to plump for some set of institutions among many sets that might put us on a quasi-Pareto or mutual-advantage frontier of welfare, a frontier far from the status quo ante of no institutions.[3]

Hume argued against the direct application of a utilitarian principle to actual cases as a shortsighted violation of principles of justice. This argument is sometimes taken as a claim against utilitarianism and for justice. In fact, it is a claim for a two-stage application of utilitarian argument. At the first stage, we decide on an institutional arrangement for resolving problems. At the second stage, we let the institution make actual decisions about allocations. Hume ([1751] 1975, 304–5) wrote:

> Cyrus, young and unexperienced, considered only the individual case before him, and reflected on a limited fitness and convenience, when he assigned the long coat to the tall boy, and the short coat to the other of smaller size. His governor instructed him better, while he pointed out more enlarged views and consequences, and in-formed his pupil of the general, inflexible rules, necessary to support general peace and order in society.

For coherent utilitarian reasons, a law of property must be established and must be applied to cases.

This is the argument of Rawls (1955) on the nature of rules and the very general argument of my institutional utilitarianism (Hardin 1988, chaps. 3 and 4). Rawls argued that there cannot be a person in the institutional position to say that a certain action, in violation of the institutional arrangements, is right.

For example, suppose that there is a particularly cruel crime sweeping the community. There cannot be someone in the criminal justice system who says that although Smith is not guilty of such a crime, still it would be better on the whole to execute Smith as though he were guilty. It would be better because the world would be better off if the actual perpetrators were dissuaded by the hanging of Smith. (I apologize for apparently constructing this silly example. It was thought to be a knock-down example in the literature against which Rawls was arguing [e.g., Carritt 1947, 65].)

A similar argument can be made about any more general normative principle. For example, fairness requires institutions for its achievement. Once those institutions are well designed and are in place to achieve it as well as possible, it would be wrong to enter, deus ex machina, and override the institutional arrangements and decisions by reallocating to make things fairer.[4]

If there is to be a later reconsideration, that possibility must be institutionalized. Indeed, in our institution of justice, we might want to make sure that there is an official locus for reconsidering certain decisions. For example, it should be possible to reconsider the death penalty for someone whose guilt might later seem to have been decided in error even by the institution's own rules, such as when a prosecutor does not reveal exonerating evidence. There should also be ways of correcting even those errors that could not have been recognized as errors at the time of the original decision, as in the recent wave of cases of exoneration of people convicted of violent crimes that the later technology of DNA evidence shows they almost certainly did not commit.[5]

The argument for ex ante design of institutional arrangements is compelling just because we could not hope to do as well without various institutions. And we can generally suppose, from a principle of insufficient reason, that ex ante everyone would benefit ordinally from having the institutions. This will very likely be a compelling argument even when the institutions in place are set up to use devices that would be ruled out by metaphysical or other complaints against them in principle. We can pragmatically put such devices in place independently of metaphysics.

Ordinal Utilitarianism

In the apparent hope of Bentham and some other early utilitarians, utilitarianism could eventually become articulate and complete in its capacity to handle choice problems in ways to enhance welfare. Because it is a theory of satisfaction of the interests of people, it must finally be subject to whatever limits there generally are on combining people's interests. The hope of Bentham, that we could construct measures of happiness and pain and perhaps even construct utility meters that could measure the levels of pleasure, pain, and, consequently, welfare of individuals, was forlorn. Instead, what we have experienced since the days of his optimistic hopes has been the increasing sophistication of welfare value theory along with the realization of its extraordinary complexity, even considered merely conceptually and analytically. The ordinal theory of the 1930s finally made sense of prices in market exchange. This realization did not completely kill the prospects of a simple, cardinal, additive utility theory, but such theory has not recovered from its failings relative to the new ordinal theory. The value theory that the ordinal revolution has given us simultaneously resolves old problems and defines new ones. *One of the new problems is the general indeterminacy of rational choice in interactive contexts.*

If rational, self-interested choice is indeterminate, we should expect to find that rational, beneficent choice is also indeterminate in many contexts. Utilitarianism in our time therefore lacks the seeming hubris of the earlier theory. But it has a realism that no other moral theory has ever had, and it is grounded in the world in which we live as no other theory is.

Some critics suppose that utilitarianism without Benthamite cardinal utility is not utilitarianism (Binmore 1991). This is a Platonic quibble that is hardly worth settling. Worse, it tends to make of utilitarianism roughly what has been made of Kantianism. In distressingly much of Kantian argument, a demonstration that Kant himself cannot be interpreted to have said something is often taken as a refutation of someone's professedly Kantian claim. As a long-current philosopher's joke has it, this turns Kantianism into cant.[6] Kant becomes like Marx: someone to be revered rather than someone to be challenged by and then to argue with. When dogmatic and fundamentally ignorant leaders of the Catholic Church made truth of claims in science depend on whether they fit with what Aristotle said, they depraved themselves and they perverted all understanding.

It is a beauty of utilitarian moral philosophy that it has more in common with the openness and debates of scientists and philosophers in fields other than ethics than with the ideological contests of many Marxians and some Kantians. It is almost inconceivable to think of utilitarianism as the doctrine of a founder, whose texts are revered, rather than as a long and varied body of original debate in which "founders" are sometimes pilloried for getting it wrong. Utilitarianism is, like all other major schools of moral theory, a movement, not a very specific theory as written down or published on a certain date. Later contributors to the movement, such as John Stuart Mill, rejected Bentham's simplistic cardinal value theory, although Mill did not yet have available the ordinal utility theory of modern economics. We do have that theory available, and we would be derelict in insisting that a moral theory be grounded in the incoherent Benthamite value theory. Many, maybe even most, twentieth-century economists who have written on moral theory or who have done moral accountings of economic issues have fully understood the ordinal value theory and nevertheless considered themselves utilitarians. They are right to do so.

The core value of utilitarianism is enhancement of welfare, somehow determined. The ways to accomplish that are not definitively settled by the very limited psychology (either of the man or of the theory) of Bentham. Bentham himself would likely have envied the advances in understanding that we enjoy, as surely Marx also would have. (I will not speak for Kant or Aristotle, but I cannot imagine that they would have been pleased to think their arguments would turn into ideologies beyond reason, debate, or criticism.) Bentham might readily have acknowledged the confusion in his writings of viewing utility both as objectively intrinsic to the objects we use and enjoy and as the subjective sum of our pleasures and pains. In his all-too-common definitional mode, he wrote: "By utility is meant *that property in any object*, whereby it tends to produce benefit, advantage, pleasure, good, or happiness [or] to prevent the happening of mischief, pain, evil, or unhappiness to the party whose interest is considered" (Bentham [1789] 1970, chap. 1, sec. 3, p. 12, emphasis added). In his richer explanatory mode, however, he developed an account of utility as the net of pleasures and pains. Presumably, he would have expanded his conception of pleasures and pains and he would have attempted to master the much later developments in value theory—alas, mostly in economic value theory, because philosophers abandoned the field about a century ago. Had these ideas been available in his time, Bentham surely would not have ignored them, although it would be unduly optimistic to suppose he would have got the issues right.

Marx did not live to see the ordinal revolution in economics, a revolution that essentially resolved the theory of value in a way that dooms any lingering attachment to a labor or other theory of intrinsic value—that is, value in objects rather than in their consumption or enjoyment. He was a voracious reader and consumer of ideas, and this idea is so powerful and beautiful that it is hard to believe he would have rejected it had it developed already in his time. He might still have argued that the working class is exploited by capitalists, but he would have had to make his argument from grounds other than the labor theory of value. One possibility might have been to argue that the class structure of industrial societies (at least in his time) did not serve mutual advantage. It seems likely that that would be a very difficult argument. A Hobbesian could say that any structure of society is better than none. Marx would have had to compare the structure not to dismal anarchy but perhaps to some alternative, maybe an ideal structure, in order to say that a mutual advantage argument yields a claim of exploitation. Most resolutions he might have offered would have required normative judgments, whereas his labor theory of value came very close to being a purely descriptive or causal theory that yielded a descriptive or causal account of exploitation.

For Marxian economists, turning Marx's views into an unquestionable ideology, so that every questioner runs the risk of being put through the trial of Galileo—with death as the potential reward in some cases—has corrupted their own work, often rendering it almost without value, not least because they attempt to found economics on a labor theory of value. Use of such economics in the communist states of the twentieth century has produced some disastrous policies, such as valuing the environment at zero because no labor went into it (rather than valuing it highly when it is in fixed and sadly limited supply, as those who used to live by fishing the nearly destroyed Aral Sea know all too well) and setting interest or discount rates so low as to overcapitalize many industrial activities. Much of that capitalization has lost its value with changing technology and with efforts to move to market organization of the society.

CONCLUDING REMARKS

Pareto's objection to cardinal, interpersonally comparable utility in economics is that it is philosophically meaningless. He typically argued that no one could make sense of the comparison of a supposed unit of my welfare and a unit of yours, although he sometimes seems to have supposed this could be done in particular cases. Hence, his objection may partly have been epistemological rather than conceptual. You and I typically know too little to make comparisons because we cannot know enough about others. Even very close lovers notoriously tend to impute their own desires to the other. Pareto's complaint against such comparison was part of his general push for greater realism in economic assumptions, many of which were stretched beyond common sense by the urge to make them complete and to mathematize them.

Consider one policy example: Good Samaritan laws. In debates over such laws, interpersonal comparisons seem to be taken seriously.[7] An example is the reputed law that on isolated stretches of the Alaskan-Canadian highway, anyone who comes upon a stranded motorist must stop to offer assistance. The argument for such a law is that all motorists would want such assistance under those circumstances and all might be in need on occasion. Hence, ex ante it is advantageous to all to have the law. This is the form of Kant's defense of altruism in general, although his argument ignores the possibility that many people might actually prefer not to have a general system of aid in place.[8] For example, many might well suppose they would typically be the ones expected to give aid and identifiable others would be those in need of aid (libertarians seem to think they are constitutionally in the former class). This is the usual problem with mutual advantage claims at the policy stage. For a policy on altruism, we might require that the conditions be very clearly unbiased ex ante, as in the remote highway case.

An oddity of a hard commonsense complaint against interpersonal comparison is that most people seem to labor under the commonsense assumption that they *do* know what it means in many contexts. For example, I might immediately grant that the welfare consequences of your major injury or disease are greater than those of my stubbed toe or common cold. It takes a relatively abstruse argument to make this comparison seem meaningless and, once the aura of splendidly refined argument has faded, the comparison regains its psychological hold for all but the most firmly dedicated theorists. These skeptical theorists, however, eventually win the day if we go so far as to claim we can add all welfare across all people to get a grand total of welfare. Before this notion, common sense also balks.

In the next chapter, I will note similarities between Bentham's invocation of cardinal utility, the use of cost-benefit analysis, and the Coase theorem. All of these devices involve focusing on collective outcomes rather than on individual choices. One might say that if it is coherent and meaningful, each of these devices is collectively rational in some sense. But they need not resolve our problem of the indeterminacy of individual choice.

Finally, note again that Bentham's move to interpersonally additive utility has strangely often been seen as the defining feature of utilitarianism (Binmore 1991). Bentham would surely have argued that the more important and genuinely defining features of his own utilitarianism were his concern with the welfare or well-being of people (see further Lyons 2000) and his focus on the need for institutions actually to organize and secure their welfare. A utilitarianism that takes modern developments in value theory to heart cannot be based on interpersonally cardinal utility but must be ordinal (Hardin 1988). Such a utilitarianism should be avowedly indeterminate just as pragmatic choice is, and for the same reasons: that strategic interaction is indeterminate and that some choice problems are stochastic.

An inherent implication of an ordinal, as opposed to a Benthamite or other cardinal, utilitarianism is that we must be more modest in our claims about the good we might do in the world. Often, our theory yields ambiguous implications or essentially no implications at all for what action we should take or what policy we should adopt. This is a conclusion that all moral theorists might well take to heart. If moral debate allowed greater play for ambiguity and indeterminacy, it would have a less assertive and dismissive quality. It would then seem more moral. It would also be more relevant.

Chapter Five

Marginal Determinacy

THE MAIN LINE of development in welfarist theory has been from Hobbesian individualist ordinalism through Benthamite interpersonally comparable cardinalism and back, through Pareto, to ordinalism. The chief problem of ordinalism has been its indeterminacy, but cardinalism does not work and cannot resolve that problem (chapter 4). In this and other respects, ordinalism is far more realistic. Its indeterminacy merely mirrors reality. Hobbes escaped this indeterminacy in his theory of the foundations of government with a nearly magic move by assuming a principle of insufficient reason to worry about details so that he could focus on the main issue of having government at all. This was a credible move for his problem, even though an analogous move in many other contexts would not be credible. In legal theory, this long tradition has culminated most recently with another magic move in the Coase theorem, which uses cardinal resources—not welfare—to resolve issues of production in a world of purely individualist ordinal values. This is probably the single cleverest move since Hobbes's own magic move in this long tradition.

The general position of all of the long line of welfarist contributors—Hobbes, Bentham, Pareto, Coase, Posner, and many others, including especially John Austin and H.L.A. Hart among those who have not been discussed here—to legal and political theory is utilitarian. Some of them have claimed not to be utilitarian or have not extensively addressed their normative assumptions. Law might, of course, be supposed to have purposes other than the enhancement of welfare. For example, Joseph Raz (1986, 226, 228) supposes its purpose should be the enhancement of autonomy. He then speaks of the virtue of the law as its efficiency—the virtue of an instrument as an instrument—because he supposes law is a means. More generally, one might argue from any moral perspective that law should be efficient in achieving whatever it is to achieve. But the tradition from Hobbes to Coase and law and economics makes efficiency the goal that law is to achieve. The efficiency is not merely of the instrument of law but rather of its effects on the society it serves. In this vision, efficiency is itself a welfarist notion because greater efficiency implies greater welfare.

For Coase, as for Pareto, efficiency is an ordinal notion. We can speak of a more efficient outcome or allocation, but we cannot speak of how much better the more efficient allocation is. In the indeterminacy of the ordinalist, welfarist program of mutual advantage, choices cannot be summarized with cardinal aggregation. Various states of affairs may be better than the current state, but no one of these may be better than the others. How, then, can we justify choosing one of these over the others? Or how can we justify saying one of them is best?

In his answer to this question, Hobbes used ignorance about the particular advantages or disadvantages of possible regimes—monarchy, oligarchy, and democracy—to allow a more or less random choice that is better than the status quo. We do not need to choose a form of government; we may simply pick one as we might pick a ball from an urn (Morgenbesser and Ullmann-Margalit 1977). Indeterminacy therefore gives Hobbes a plausible solution while it gets back in the way for Pareto with his partially more advanced Hobbesian views. His views are more advanced technically, but Pareto deals only with allocation of what we already have, while Hobbes was concerned far more with arranging life to enable far greater production. Coase resolves further indeterminacy introduced by production with his cardinal money measure that yields ordinal information about individual preferences or interests.

INDETERMINACY ON THE FRONTIER

The static principle of Pareto improvement is somewhat indeterminate because it cannot tell us which of many choices, all of which are superior to the status quo, we should collectively make. As argued in chapter 3, it therefore does not give a prescription for individual choice. We might suppose that introducing concern with dynamic efficiency would compound the indeterminacy. The Coase theorem explains why this conclusion need not follow. In essence, the theorem says that no matter what the assignment of legal rights to use a particular property or resource, it will be used by the producer who can achieve the highest net income from production—unless transaction costs swamp the potential gains from transacting to reassign the use of the rights. Why? Because the titular owner of the rights will bargain them away to a more efficient producer for a relevant share of the greater income that that producer can achieve (Coase [1960] 1988, 97–104). Coase essentially dismisses any claim that the allocation of property rights is determinate for production and argues that it is market return that is determinative. Once we have maximized production, we still have Pareto's problem of how to allocate the extra benefits from our move to the production frontier.

Recall the example from chapter 1. The total net profits from a farmer's crops and a rancher's cattle are a function of their sales value less the costs of raising them. This total is essentially a cardinal value in, say, dollars. Suppose these profits could be increased by letting the cattle roam over part of the farmer's land, destroying some of her crops, but that the farmer has the right to fence her land against the cattle. The two then have an interest in striking a deal that allows the cattle to roam over part of the farmer's land (Coase [1960] 1988, 95, 99). In this deal, part of the extra profits the rancher makes from the farmer's not fencing his cattle off her land go to the farmer as compensation for lost profits from her damaged crops, and the two split the remaining extra profits. Hence, each can be made ordinally better off by making the deal.

We might suppose this move turns money into a cardinal utility or welfare measure. It does not. It merely assumes that, all else being equal, more money is better than less for every individual. Suppose we face two (or more) outcomes. The market values in outcome *A* are higher than those in outcome *B*. Hence, in *A* there are more dollars to be shared, and all parties can in principle be made better off (transaction costs may be prohibitive). This is strictly an ordinal claim; or, rather, it is strictly an ordinal claim *for each party* taken alone. It assumes nothing about the total value to each party; it merely assumes that each party can be made better off. *The move from fewer dollars to more can be made as a move of mutual advantage.* That is why we can generally expect it to be made if its benefits are recognized and if the costs of transaction do not block it.

For present purposes, we may distinguish four main assumptions of Coase: First, Coase's theorem trades on the fact-value distinction. There is nothing inherently good or right about the way a burden is to be shared merely in the facts of the matter (Coase [1960] 1988, 119–33). What makes, for example, action *X* a nuisance? Surprisingly, much writing in nuisance law has ignored this question. Why? Perhaps many writers are closet deontological libertarians who think they know when property and related rights are being violated. The sadly untalented drummer across the street from me as I write this is, to me, a nuisance. But to the law he is not, unless he continues past midnight. And in any case, he is a nuisance to me only because I happen to live here. If someone else lived here, he might be applauded. Coase is evidently a legal positivist— as was Hobbes—who thinks of rights as matters of law or legal rules. Hence, although we might use injunction against some activity for efficiency reasons, we may not have a moral reason of right to use it, contrary to common implicit assumption.

Second, the core normative content of Coase's theorem is that of Hobbes, Hume, and Pareto: mutual advantage as the collective implication of self-interest. If one outcome is more productive than another, we can all be made better off by reaching it with relevant compensations. The Coase theorem is not indeterminate about our collective pattern of production—we will end up where the total value of production is greatest. But it is indeterminate about how we will share the benefits of our greater productivity. Hence, its indeterminacy is that of Pareto's principles. It is indeterminate about the allocation of the final profit that we have after settling on maximum production (Coase [1960] 1988, 100).

Third, we have to look at costs and benefits to all concerned in an interaction. This follows straightforwardly from Coase's implicit assumption of mutual advantage as his underlying principle of justification. But we do not simply add these costs and benefits. We look only to ordinal judgments by the relevant parties without recourse to interpersonal comparisons. Coase's examples are often two-party interactions with no external effects on other parties assumed (Coase [1960] 1988, 98). But if there are such effects, these must be taken into account.

Fourth, we have to take real-world constraints of transaction costs and political-legal institutions into consideration. If transaction costs are nil, *all systems of entitlements will lead to efficient production.* If transaction costs are low, all parties to an interaction might easily be brought to understand that there could be a mutual advantage resolution. But if transaction costs are high enough, there may be no prospect of improving on a status quo allocation of rights and the lower level of production that follows from failure to contract for uses of the property that would have greater productivity.

For many law and economics scholars, a corollary follows from these. Because information and bargaining costs may be high, incomplete contracts may be efficient and may require court resolution to fill in the gaps (Polinsky 1989, 27–38). Note that this corollary is analogous to Hobbes's move to justify government, which will then resolve such problems as marginal gaps in our initial design. Similarly, in many works, James Buchanan and various coauthors argue that we may agree ex ante on a constitutional device or procedure for handling marginal problems on which we would not agree (see, for example, Brennan and Buchanan 1985). More generally, for all of life's interactions with legally unanticipated conflicts, we might want court resolutions that establish principles of resolution from efficiency considerations.

There are three critical aspects of Coase's device that should be noted. First, for the device to work there must be a going market with prices for the products at issue. That is to say, Hobbes's problem of social order must already have been resolved and there must be relatively solid legal institutions for handling property rights and other issues. Coase is dealing entirely at the margin of an extant economy.

Second, we cannot represent the Coasean allocation on a Pareto diagram. The actual range of allocations will run from all of our net profit from renegotiating the use of our rights going to you to all of it going to me. The net, however, no matter how it is shared, is a constant sum. This would be representable as a straight line in total income at a slope of minus one. Because income need not translate uniformly into welfare, the Pareto frontier in welfare need not be a straight line. Indeed, unlike the income frontier, the Paretian welfare frontier is not cardinal.[1] All we can say about the welfare frontier, then, is that, ceteris paribus, the higher your share of our net income from reallocating our production rights, the greater your welfare. As always, ordinal improvements entail cardinal increases if the latter are meaningful.[2] Coase's device was not designed to reach the Pareto frontier of efficient allocation of what we already have but to reach the production frontier for the given resources, such as land, and to do this to the mutual advantage of the parties. *Because the allocation of the extra profits from increased production is only a matter of mutual advantage, it is not determinate.* We cannot say how it will be shared between the parties.

And third, Coasean resolution maximizes productive income only subject to the constraint that the parties choose to trade off various other things for income. Income has value only as a resource for consumptions. Hence, neither party to a Coasean transaction over the use of property rights could reasonably neglect the effects of reallocation on consumptions in general. For example, if the farmer is willing to pay a premium for peace and quiet, the available net gain from higher production may be substantially less than if the farmer did not value such consumption highly.

How does Coase's resolution of collective interactions differ from Hobbes's justification of political order? Hobbes uses ignorance about the particular advantages or disadvantages of possible regimes to allow a more or less random choice of possible forms of government that is better than the status quo. For him, the difference between any two forms of government "is scarce sensible" in comparison to the difference between any working government and either anarchy or civil war (Hobbes [1651] 1968, chap. 18, p.[94] 238). This too is a strictly ordinal claim, not a cardinal one. Indeterminacy gets in the way for Pareto. It is irrelevant to Hobbes, largely for epistemological or social-scientific reasons in his assumption of substantial ignorance about future prospects under variant forms of government. Coase resolves indeterminacies that might be introduced by alternative regimes of production. He does so with his cardinal money measure, which yields ordinal information about individual preferences or interests.

Marginal versus Fundamental Values

Again, note one perplexing implication of Coase's resolution: it is inherently marginalist. Hobbes addressed the big, fundamental issue of how to justify government in general or even a particular government. Coase addresses the issue of justifying a particular resolution of a marginal problem that might arise under government. There are no dollars with which to perform Coase's magic back under Hobbes's conditions. Dollars follow Hobbes's resolution; they do not precede it.[3] There is a sense, then, in which once Hobbes's general program to establish government is done, Coase may build on it to resolve more detailed questions in the economy and in actual law.

Indeed, Coase builds not only on the existence of government but also on the development of enough knowledge to make it plausible to suppose we might improve things, even if only at the margin. Hobbes may not have known whether monarchy or oligarchy was the better form of government, but we may often know that assigning production contrary to apparent ownership rights would lead to greater productivity.

One might even claim against Hobbes that we are able to justify only marginal adjustments in government. But Hobbes's assessment of the goodness of government, as defined by the interests of individuals, is conceptually coherent. Indeed, in some cases it may even be empirically meaningful, such as when a society that has fallen into murderous chaos is brought back to order by external intervention. In such a case, we might not be able to say that the intervention brings about the best of all resolutions, but we might be relatively confident that it works to the mutual advantage of virtually all concerned in the previously chaotic state.

Consider two relatively simple examples of a mutual advantage intervention to create order in an anarchic context that is murderous. Among the Yanomamö, an acephalous society along the Brazilian-Venezuelan border, and the Fore of Highland New Guinea, there was a culture of incessant warfare and revenge murder that they themselves could not stop. According to C. R. Hallpike (1973), the Yanomamö and other such societies "engage in warfare because among other reasons they cannot stop, not because they necessarily as a culture derive any benefit from fighting. In the absence of any central authority they are condemned to fight for ever, other conditions remaining the same, since for any group to cease defending itself would be suicidal. In some cases of this type the people have no real desire to continue fighting, and may welcome outside pacification."[4]

Hence, there is substantial social organization with genuine control over individuals. Among the Fore of Highland New Guinea, external intervention that was not very forceful, that played little more than a signaling role was sufficient to bring peace. "The warfare was not liked, and the distant presence of but a single [British] patrol officer and a handful of native police was grasped as an excuse to cease" (Sorrenson 1972; see further Colson 1974, 62–89). In the difficult terrain of New Guinea, the single patrol officer was days away from people who nevertheless seized on his presence to be peaceable. The problem could be reduced to a signaling problem because there was immediately a single plausible resolution of it when the colonial power arrived on the scene. These examples were almost a picture of the state of nature as conceived by Hobbes. The chief difference is that the fighting is not anarchically individual by individual but at least moderately organized community by community.

As Hobbes presented it, Hobbesian efficiency provides a justification *of* law—that is, of the whole system of law—as in these two anthropological cases. Coasean efficiency, in its law-and-economics corollary, provides, rather, arguments for justification *in* law—that is, for the specific content of particular laws or court rulings. Hobbes moves from violent anarchy to mutually beneficial order. Coase shows that bringing in dynamic concern with production need not compound Paretian allocative indeterminacy with Hobbesian dynamic indeterminacy, although he does so only at the margin. Both Hobbes and Coase are concerned with production, not merely with allocation of what exists. In that respect, they are quite different from Pareto, who did not successfully integrate production into his economics (Kirman 1987, 806). Indeed, it is their concern with production that gives them their resolutions, although Hobbes also required great skepticism about one bit of social science (judgment of whether one form of government would better serve our interests than another would) and great confidence in another (the high probability that even efforts at reform would lead to civil war) to achieve his result.

Law and economics, contemporary price theory, and the indifference-curve utility theory are generally about issues at the margin of a background of general arrangements. Hobbes addressed this background and not the marginal issues. From roughly Hume forward, most discussion has been at the margin. Among later writers discussed here, Rawls ([1971] 1999) is unusual in attempting to establish principles for the background of general arrangements. Henry Sidgwick (perhaps the greatest utilitarian) argued that we do not know enough to start from fundamentals; we can only talk intelligently about improvements on what exists (Sidgwick 1907, 473–74).[5] John Dewey ([1929] 1960, chap. 9) and the pragmatists shared this view. Dewey said that the most we can expect of our efforts is that they bring improvement in our state of affairs, not that they bring us to or nearer to some well-defined final goal.

Lon Fuller also shared Hobbes's full vision of mutual advantage coupled with limited reason. On our limited reason, he said, we need not know the morally best state of affairs in order to judge one state better than another. "And it is on this common sense view that we build our institutions and practices" (Fuller [1964] 1969, 32; also see 10–12). Elsewhere he argued for what he called the "coordination function of law," that law serves mutual advantage (Fuller [1969] 1981, 231–32; also see Fuller [1964] 1969, 9). Fuller was concerned not with whether you and I make an exchange but whether if we wish to or stand to gain from doing so, the law will facilitate our doing so. Contract law, tort law, and much else are, in this sense, among the facilitative branches of the law.[6]

In all these systems, a specific case that is decided at law is likely to go against one party or the other, or it must strike a compromise over their conflicting interests. This choice cannot be merely efficient in the sense of mutually advantageous. It is only from an ex ante point of view that the decision can be considered efficient, and then only if the distribution of parties to relevantly similar interactions is not known (Hobbesian ignorance makes for agreement).

Hence, the *resolution* cannot directly be argued on efficiency grounds; rather, the *system* that permits and accomplishes resolutions is efficient (Coase [1960] 1988, 141–42).

Hobbes's odd commitment to absolutism fits this institutionalist perspective. He virtually refused to make arguments at the margin of a going political order. In his system, marginal changes were the full prerogative of the sovereign. This recourse to the sovereign is analogous to the ultimate recourse of the institutionalist to the institution for deciding cases. The institutionalist might allow revision of the law through common-law or appellate courts. But there is no way to justify the status quo on which Coase works—except perhaps as Hobbes might, by arguing that the expected costs to each and every one of us of our attempting to move to a new system or distribution are too great.

For exchange relations, justification from mutual advantage might seem to make sense a case at a time. But what we must actually want in law are general principles for handling and enforcing contracts. If the need for enforcement arises in any given contract relation, then the parties no longer face the prospect of a resolution that serves their mutual advantage. The mutual advantage justification of the law of contracts or of any of its principles is inherently at the system level and is prior to its use in an actual contract.

To see the system-level nature of the argument from the mutual advantage of law most clearly, however, consider the way torts are handled, both in law and in law and economics. In a tort interaction, at least one of the parties has suffered a harm, and the law of torts determines how the costs are to be borne by the parties. Can we argue from mutual advantage here? Surely not at the individual-case level. But tort law can be treated as analogous to contract law in that there is an expected gain to all from having certain activities available despite their tendency to produce harmful side effects, such as auto accident injuries.

We can serve mutual advantage ex ante by adopting an efficient rule for tort cases. What we all would agree to is to be able, for example, to drive our cars with a regime for handling the allocation of the side costs. When proponents of law and economics argue for the Coasean corollary—assignment of property rights on the basis of their productive efficiency *in the face of transaction costs*—the mutual advantage argument is strictly ex ante. Similarly, we can get a mutual advantage justification of a tort regime ex ante. But when the regime is actually brought to bear on a tort interaction, one party may lose from the application of the tort remedy.

Does the system-level justification really fit a mutual advantage argument? Yes, but only if everyone is likely to be more or less randomly on either side of the tort rule. If we are systematically divided into two classes with different but interacting behaviors, there may be no mutual advantage rule for governing our interactions. For example, suppose I am almost always going to be a driver and you are always going to be a pedestrian. Now our interactions all have the character of the single interaction; they are not statistically random. There are no balancing interactions in which I have the pedestrian's interests and you have the driver's interests. Each actual settlement is a pure conflict between two parties to a tort loss, and the sum of all settlements is also a pure conflict between two distinctly defined classes of parties to all the tort losses. Hence, a rule that lets the loss lie where it falls so long as the driver is driving reasonably might systematically assign some of the interactive costs of driving to nondrivers. Note that this issue is further complicated by the possibility that your evaluation of a given physical loss might dramatically differ from mine, even though the physical damage done is the same under some meaningful description. For example, your violinist's hand may be worth much more than my word processor's hand (for discussion, see Calabresi 1985).

Much argument in law and economics is only implicitly grounded in justification from mutual-advantage. For example, discussions of torts generally seem to take for granted that it is okay to do such things as drive cars despite the virtually certain knowledge that doing so may put us at risk of killing or injuring someone. The issue is not whether I should go to jail for having driven at all, but whether I should help to make you whole after our accident. This may recall hoary discussions of the doctrine of double effect. My intention when I drive is to get to a party, not to kill the person I might accidentally hit along the way. Hence I might do no wrong if indeed I do accidentally kill someone. This is, again, the nature of strategic interaction. My action is in fact a strategy, from which many varied outcomes may follow.

Coase gives a mutual-advantage grounding of a version of this principle of the doctrine of double effect without becoming entangled in the simplistic causal action theory of that doctrine. In Coase's causal theory, I could do harm to you only if I am not acting merely on my own but am interacting with you. But that means your harm was jointly produced by us, even though your only part in the joint causation may have been to be standing on a particular bit of sidewalk. If we think your harm was jointly caused, it is odd to attribute sole moral fault to me. I have only joint causal effect. Yet much of tort law has been a law of fault finding. On a Coasean or law and economics account it is eminently plausible that everything I did was right and everything you did was right, and yet the joint outcome of our actions was a grievous harm to one of us. The point of the law is to balance our interests in the face of such strategic interactions and, arguably, to give us incentives to reduce the incidence of such harmful interactions thereafter.

Transaction Costs

If their transaction costs are high, Coase's farmer may not reach agreement with the rancher on how to handle their arrangement in order to produce greater income to both of them. For example, either partner in the deal could try to conceal true costs and benefits in order to extract a larger share of the net gains, and both parties might have to expend egregious costs in legal fees. Such fees in contract negotiations might be a rough proxy for transaction costs in a legalistic society such as the United States. These transaction costs might be indeterminate in many contexts, so that finding out what they are is tantamount to expending them. Hence, we might expect less success in resolving Coasean marginal problems than we would get if transaction costs were merely transparent and predictable. Because they often are not, they can be used in bargaining, which is to say that the uncertainty about them may increase them. They can therefore introduce their own bit of indeterminacy in the interactive choice.

CONCLUDING REMARKS

In his vision of dynamic efficiency, Hobbes ran welfarist and resourcist views together. Increasing efficiency ipso facto increases welfare. The efficiency he wanted is just a matter of greater welfare individual by individual. Coase's Theorem also is resourcist in its move to prices and income. But this is only a temporary device for getting to welfare. Posner's move in his principle of wealth maximization (chapter 4) is far more complex, and perhaps less coherent. It blends welfare considerations into the prima facie resourcist notion of wealth. Some such move may finally be conceptually required of all of these theories, because consumptions, welfare, and resources trade off against each other or are mutually constituted (see further Hardin 2001).

The great trick of Coase is to convert general income from higher production into money shares that can be allocated to make all relevant individuals ordinally better off. Income is treated cardinally and interpersonally, although it has no value except as a means. Nevertheless, the welfare gains of individuals that come from gains in income are still ordinal and need not be interpersonally comparable. Hence, we can, by using higher money income as a device, reach mutually beneficial outcomes. This was already the early trick of a market economy in which money allows trades to become generalized without the need for direct matching of substantive demands and supplies between particular parties. *It is a mistake both in the judgment of the market with money and in Coasean monetary assessments to focus on money as somehow the real value of what is going on. It is merely a means to the allocation of values, generally welfare values.*

As noted earlier, law and economics scholars have built on the Coase Theorem to advocate ex ante creation of institutions to resolve problems thereafter, especially in response to the problem of transaction costs. Hobbes made a similar move, but in response to the likely conflict over laws and their enforcement and over what we would today call policies. Both moves are instances of the ex ante creation of institutions that then will make decisions we could not have made, as discussed in chapter 8. It is such mechanical imposition of determinacy by institutions that can finally resolve some of the remaining problems of indeterminacy of our theories.

Finally, note parallels and differences between the Coase Theorem, the use of cardinal utility, and cost-benefit analysis (the latter two as discussed in chapter 4). In invoking cardinally additive utility, Bentham could determine the final outcome of any collective project we might have. In Coase's Theorem, we can determine the overall production independently of the ownership rights. In neither case, however, can we determine the allocation of the overall benefits that these theories stipulate. Both theories can, in principle, tell us what is our total (of utility or money) for allocation, but they do not fully constrain how that total is distributed among us. They are indeterminate at the point of allocation. Bentham's device of cardinal welfare can violate mutual advantage; Coase's device is to use cardinal money to achieve mutual advantage. Hence, Coase's device is ordinalist in its implications for welfare.

Bentham's move does not work in any case because the idea of cardinal utility is not coherent. Coase's move does work because it uses money, which can meaningfully be added. The assumptions of cost-benefit analysis seem similar to Coase's assumptions in that they involve monetary calculation. Cost-benefit analysis, however, reverses the order of application of cardinal and ordinal principles. Coase uses the cardinal value of what is produced (as measured by market prices). The use of cost-benefit analysis presumes that we would all be ordinally better off ex ante if we could use cost-benefit analysis for specific classes of policy decisions. This presumption can be true even though there need be no sense in which our monetary assignments of costs and benefits to the individuals affected by a policy are compelling. Hence, the cardinalization of costs and benefits is largely a sham, although it is used for good effect.

Chapter Six

Rules for Determinacy

THE OLDEST and in many ways the most simplistic device for dealing with indeterminacy in social interaction is to develop and impose rules for behavior in certain contexts only. At issue here are rules such as those in moral theory that proscribe or prescribe certain actions. Such rules are inherently clouded by the difficulty of defining actions in contexts of strategic interaction. The action in many contexts is a joint action, and few if any of the rules that are commended to us govern joint action. A major class of moral theory, Kantianism, issues rules for behavior, even imperative rules that it would be seriously, morally wrong for a Kantian not to heed. Such theory is called deontology, a term coined by Bentham to cover the general category of "moral science" but now, oddly, reserved for theories that focus on actions rather than on consequences, although Bentham was the supreme consequentialist. The actions at issue in Kantian morality are individual, not collective or joint, actions.

There are many kinds of rule. There are many rules that are straightforwardly rational and interest-serving in a quite determinate way, such as the rules of the road that merely coordinate us. And there are many others that are essentially pragmatic rules, such as a rule of thumb to plant after a certain date, that might be scientifically justified as at least approximately correct with further knowledge. But some rules are strictly rules for managing social traffic and relations in the face of likely conflict. Many of these today would be considered moral rules, and they descend from custom, religion, and even— rarely—moral theory. In addition to Kantian moral theory, intuitionist moral theory, which dominated Anglo-Saxon philosophical ethics through much of the early-twentieth century, commonly is about rules for action.

Many moral rules, from both the Kantian and intuitionist schools, such as "don't lie," make eminently good sense even on a pragmatic analysis, so long as they are not ironclad and unforgiving. In some societies, moralizing such essentially pragmatic rules might help to enforce them as guides for behavior, all to the benefit of those, such as children and others who are shortsighted, on whom they are enforced. Many, perhaps most, of such rules in common use today appear quite clearly to be utilitarian in the mutual advantage sense that following them improves social life for one and all most of the time. As a device for overcoming indeterminacy, however, they are little better than living with indeterminacy or even pretending it away. No catalog of moral rules comes even vaguely close to covering the range of possible actions that must matter to us and that affect us deeply.

Rules are, like some of the other devices considered here, a great simplifying device. They say, more or less, that these are the norms we must follow and anything more than this is not as obligatory. Indeed, there is generally thought to be a distinction in the force even of those rules we do have. There are minatory rules—rules that threaten punishment for their violation; and there are hortatory rules—rules that exhort (but commonly do not require) us to do better. "Do not lie" is usually seen as a minatory rule. "Love thy neighbor" is at best a hortatory rule, indeed, one that often exhorts us to go beyond our possibilities, so that our failure to live by it cannot plausibly be overcome by the threat of punishment.

The striking fact of many, maybe essentially all, such rules is that they are massively indeterminate in the senses that, taken as a set, they are often contradictory, they give an incomplete guide to behavior, and they commonly would lead us to harm, not good, if we followed them. Without some kind of correcting judgment of the effects of following certain rules, they would often be disastrous. This is true because even though a concern for our own pragmatic interests is seldom among the rules explicitly, such a concern would be severely overrun by simplistic rules that might seem to make sense most of the time—but not all of the time. I will break discussion here into two parts: rules and principles. Perhaps the second part should be in the singular, because the only principle I address is Kant's principle that we may not use another as a means only, that we must always treat another as an end in herself or himself. I will follow these discussions with a brief account of the institutional nature of policy resolutions.

Kant and Kantian arguments also come centrally into the discussion of rules, because, as noted, Kantian moral theory essentially gives us rules for behavior. One might be more catholic and take up rules more generally. But most of the so-called moral rules are intuitionist claims, and it is of little interest to consider them (see further Hardin 1988, 178–91). Moreover, most of the compelling rules of ordinary morality tend to have found favor with Kant and his followers, so that they are not entirely left out of consideration. (It is a remarkable feat of moral theorists typically to reach conclusions that are very close to ordinary popular morality in their own time and place. The only part of moral theory that cannot come close to popular conceptions is the scaffolding from which rules or principles for behavior are supposedly deduced. Alas, for philosophers, that is where all the credit is earned.)

Moral theories fall into two somewhat artificial modal categories. Many are primarily theories directed to personal behavior in face-to-face and small-number interactions. And many, while partly personal, are distinguished by their strong commitment to social and political concerns. Twentieth-century moral theory in the Anglo-Saxon world was almost entirely personal in the seven decades before Rawls's *Theory of Justice*. The turn to personal morality afflicted theories as different as Kantianism and utilitarianism. Kant himself addressed issues of international peace, government, and jurisprudence, although his discussions of these are arguably not genuinely extensions of his moral theory, which is entirely at the individual level and is about individual actions. More critically, early utilitarians had been conspicuously concerned foremost with institutions and governments. Indeed, utilitarianism was the reigning moral theory of law in the Anglo-Saxon world until the rise of rights-talk in recent decades (Hart 1979). In this chapter, I focus on personal morality that is framed as rules for behavior.

To speak of determinacy inherently suggests at least a partial focus on outcomes or consequences. My action is indeterminate because it does not determine a specific outcome, as it usually does when my action is merely flipping a light switch. This is typically a problem with interactive choice and with choice in stochastic contexts, in both of which I might have some ex ante expectations of the likely outcomes of my actions, although I would not have determinate expectations. Deontological moral theories typically insist that all we should judge morally is actions or act-kinds independently of their consequences. Such a theory is prima facie problematic if we think determinacy is problematic. Deontologists might therefore reject the arguments here as coming from outside their theory, rather than from within it. That position is, of course, correct. But the focus on indeterminacy may nevertheless help to clarify the force of the commitment to following rules independently of their causal implications. It requires an astonishing commitment in the face of the indeterminacy of act-kinds in contexts of stochastic problems and of strategic interaction and therefore of the indeterminacy of any theory that stipulates the rightness or wrongness of particular act-kinds. Rejecting any concern with indeterminacy makes such theory otherworldly.

Moreover, significant institutions are inherently constructed of interactions of many people and any actions or policies of an institution are the product of extensive interaction. A deontological account of the rightness of act-kinds within or by any substantial institution must therefore be a weirdly complex contraption that would give even Rube Goldberg difficulties. The rescue of some theories by the device of passing their choices off to institutions, as discussed in chapter 8, is unlikely to work well for a resolutely deontological theory of act-kinds.

RULES

The two most articulate discussions of rules are in the Kantian tradition, in which the rules are supposedly derived from more general principles, and in the rule-utilitarian tradition, in which the rules are similarly derived from a more general principle, the principle of welfare enhancement. I will discuss their difficulty in the face of strategic interaction or a stochastic physical world, which are the sources of indeterminacy in this book. Virtually all moral rules seem to address actions or act-kinds. These days they are usually deontological rather than consequentialist, so that they are supposed to be inviolable. There have been discussions of utilitarian rules that are similar to pragmatic rules of thumb, which are generally good guides for action but which are occasionally subject to being overruled by more careful consideration of their effects in particular contexts. Such rules are not at issue here.

There is an immediately obvious problem with rules seen in the context of choices in social interaction, which is what most moral rules are meant to govern.[1] The problem is that the choice of a strategy in a game bears little resemblance to an act-kind such as moralists wish to govern with their rules. A favorite example in philosophy is Kant's claim that it is wrong to lie no matter what the supposed consequences of the lie. It is only the purity of the moral action of telling the truth and the impurity of lying that matters. To make his view incontrovertibly clear, he asserted that we should not even lie to an intended murderer who asks us if his intended victim is in our house. Even though it might mean the intended victim's immediate death, Kant supposes one should truthfully answer that the victim is in the house. Even for a Protestant Prussian of Kant's time, that seems to be an unduly formalistic view.

Kant was challenged in his view by Benjamin Constant, who proposed the example of the intended murderer. Constant argued that a moral injunction here clearly turns on how immoral are the circumstances one faces. Kant ([1797] 1909, 365, final emphasis added) replied at length in print, concluding with what may be one of the clearest, most intransigently deontological, anti-consequentialist arguments ever framed:

> we must not understand [the issue as one of] the danger of *doing harm* (accidentally), but of *doing wrong*; and this would happen if the duty of veracity, which is quite unconditional, and constitutes the supreme condition of justice in utterances, were made conditional and subordinate to other considerations; and, although by a certain lie I in fact do no wrong to any person [such as the intending murderer], yet I infringe the principle of justice in regard to all indispensably necessary statements *generally* (I do wrong formally, though not materially); *and this is much worse than to commit an injustice to any individual.*

There are two remarkable aspects of Kant's view here that should be mentioned. First, one may note that almost no one other than Kant seems to have thought his radical principle on lying follows from his larger moral theory. Indeed, W. I. Matson ([1954] 1967, 336), a sympathetic critic who defends Kant's larger moral theory against Kant's grotesque judgment in this instance, thinks the "repellent fanaticism" of this passage merely shows that Kant lived too long as a philosopher.[2] One might respond that, on the contrary, Kant did not live long enough as a philosopher to see the world we know. Imagine anyone's arguing against a rescuer who lies to a Nazi inspector in order to protect the Jewish family hidden in her cellar. To say that the rescuer's lie is *much worse than to commit an injustice to any individual* is preposterous and profoundly depraved, so depraved as to make one turn in disgust from anyone who would make such an argument in this context.

On this depraved principle, Oskar Schindler was profoundly immoral for the skein of lies he must have had to tell during the years of his risky rescue efforts to protect many people against the extermination policies of the Nazis. This conclusion is so outrageous that one might be forgiven for getting angry and wanting to shake sense into dear old Kant. If that is morality, why would we want it? It is utterly indecent. Nevertheless, the rule against lying is analytically a good example for discussion here, in part because it exemplifies very well the incoherent notion of it *as merely a simple action*, and in part because perhaps more ink has been spilled on arguing its merits than on arguing any other rule except plausibly the rule to keep promises.[3] It is an astonishing and depressing fact that these two matters have held such a central place in moral debate. If these two matters loom so large at the core of morality, we do not need morality and we should tell the moralists to leave us alone while we tend to more important matters.

One particularly bad but commonplace defense of an inviolable rule, such as that against lying, is a kind of generalization argument. We might ask, "If we could cause everybody to tell the truth all the time by putting sodium Pentothal in the water supply, would we want to do it?" We could say yes to this query but still recognize that in an actual moment of my having to decide (without the influence of sodium Pentothal) whether to tell some brute the truth, my best action is to lie. One might also answer NO to the generalization query very generally for the reason that we would think life with the constant rudeness of the truth would be ugly, as Thomas Nagel and others convincingly argue (Nagel 1998; Campbell 2001; Nyberg 1993; for a contrary view, see Bok 1978). I think that both the exception in the first answer and the whole of the second answer are compelling, so that the defense of an inviolable rule against lying from a generalization argument is doubly bad.[4] (Other inviolable rules generally fail the first test here, but they need not fail the Nagel test.)[5]

Second, one should note that the issue here is far more general in its import than merely for lying, and in this respect the lesson to be drawn is relevant to any theory that prescribes (or proscribes) kinds of acts per se. The more general issue is the relation between actions relatively narrowly defined and the consequences that result from them. It is characteristic of *strategic actions that their character and definition is typically supposed to follow from their likely results* or, more commonly, their likely range of potential results. I do X in order to achieve C. It is almost impossible to formulate many policy statements without formulating them in terms of their intended consequences. To formulate them exclusively in terms of the actions permissible under them would ordinarily be quite cumbersome and irrelevant. The point of policies is generally to effect consequences. It is probably at least in part for this reason that deontological theory has seldom been about policies or institutional actions more generally. Applying a strictly deontological moral theory to government would lead almost exclusively to procedural conclusions because it is about what we can do and not about what results we achieve.

Of course, a deontological moral theory that focused exclusively on kinds of actions, rather than on the results of actions, need not moralize everything, so that many actions, as such, might be neither required nor prohibited by a particular theory, while many others, such as lying, might be rigidly governed by the theory. One cannot make much sense of a moral injunction to vaccinate or not to vaccinate someone without tying it to the actual ex ante assessment of the effects it is supposed to have.[6] (In chapter 3 I discussed vaccination as a problem for mutual-advantage theory; here I consider it as a problem for deontological rule theories). Hence, one cannot have a sensible principle on vaccination in the way one might have a general principle on lying as somehow right or wrong independently of its likely consequences. Of course, this conclusion is quite general in its import. It applies not only to vaccination but also to a vast class of large-scale policy problems and choices stochastic and otherwise.

Moral theories that persuasively proscribe such act-kinds as killing, lying, and so forth, cannot transparently be applied to such act-kinds as those that put some at risk of great harm for the sake of slight or even great benefit for others. Hence, they cannot transparently apply to many policy issues. Indeed, they cannot even transparently apply to the act-kinds that fill quotidian life. Such stochastic choice issues are at the core of public policy and applied ethics and of practical personal life. Any credible moral theory must master this problem before it can speak confidently to us on such issues.

A sensible policy on vaccination is inherently consequentialist. It may even be ultimately utilitarian. One whose moral theory is based on act-kinds need not disagree with utilitarian prescriptions in such a policy issue. Such a theorist could concede vaccination prescriptions to utilitarian considerations and, with utilitarians, conclude that the act-kind of vaccinating someone is made right or wrong by its general fit with the policy. But then the distinctive character of that person's theory may have no role in the moral evaluation of policies on vaccination and other stochastic problems. This would be a hard lesson. It would very nearly drop such a morality from all concern with public policy. A standard response of deontologists to consequentialism is that it is wrong because it allows no other consideration into a decision. They say deontology can admit consequentialist reasons when these clearly trump. In matters of public policy they generally trump. Again, it is hard to imagine a point to policy in many contexts other than to effect consequences.

A KANTIAN PRINCIPLE

Let us consider two problems dicussed earlier in different contexts in which blinkered focus on individual actions makes little sense of our purposes. The first, which is possibly just a stochastic problem of dealing with nature, is the recently successful program of eradication of smallpox in the wild, which is to say, in natural contexts of spontaneous infection through exposure to others with smallpox. The second is the system of nuclear deterrence that, until recently, in the antagonism between the Soviet Union and the United States, threatened the potential destruction of all humankind. That system worked through influencing the actions of others, so that it was primarily a problem of strategic interaction—although there was also a real problem of devastating accidental warfare that would not have been intentional. It is instructive to begin with the strategically simple problem of smallpox eradication because that program might yet have consequences far worse than the continuation of sporadic epidemics of smallpox.

Let us back up the inoculation program by slightly over two centuries to when Edward Jenner performed the first cowpox vaccination to protect against smallpox. He had noticed that dairymaids who got cowpox from cows never got smallpox in subsequent epidemics. Cowpox is a mild variant of the many pox diseases—and in fact a variant that could more accurately be called rodent pox, because cows get it from rodents, and only rarely. In 1796 Jenner therefore deliberately inoculated a boy with cowpox. A few months later he scratched the boy's arm with pus from a smallpox patient. The boy did not get the illness. This experiment presumably would not get past any ethics review board today. But was it wrong in its time? Given the state of knowledge in his time, Jenner had few devices available to him with which to attack the awful scourge of smallpox, possibly the most hideous disease in human history and often epidemic in Jenner's time (Hopkins 2000). One might also note that that boy may well have survived a later epidemic because he was vaccinated. Jenner, incidentally, recognized that the eventual implication of his discovery would be "the annihilation of the Small Pox, the most dreadful scourge of the human species." The high-sounding term, *vaccination*, was coined by Jenner from the mundane Latin word for "cow" (Preston 1999, 52).

In Massachusetts in 1721, two generations before Jenner's medical experiment, Zabdiel Boylston used live pox to inoculate 247 people, his son and friends, against smallpox. Six died, or 1 in 41. Boylston was reviled. In a subsequent epidemic, the remaining 241 of his vaccinees survived, while 1 in 7 of the rest of the population died (Koshland 1985; *Encyclopedia Britannica* 2: 213). Inoculation, even of Boylston's crude form, seems to have posed the lesser ex ante risk. (Of course, he was performing an experiment in a state of such ignorance that he could not have known how good the odds were.) If it was random chance which of Boylston's vaccinees died of smallpox and which would have died from the later epidemic, then most or all of those who died in the inoculation would have survived had they not been vaccinated, while thirty to forty others in the group would have died. Jenner is today considered the father of vaccination, but Boylston preceded him by many decades.

Note that many actual inoculation programs are not so different from Boylston's. Some of those inoculated contract the disease against which we try to protect them or are otherwise harmed by the vaccination. And those who get the disease from the inoculation might not have got it or might not have suffered as much from exposure to an actual epidemic instead of the vaccine. If about six-sevenths of the population survive a typical epidemic, presumably something at least approaching six-sevenths of those who died from vaccination would have survived the epidemic if not vaccinated. Ex post, at least, we have clearly used those people to gain protection for others, many others.

Because it is live, inoculation with the Sabin vaccine against polio yields some herd immunity—that is, protection of those who are not vaccinated but who are exposed to the attenuated virus. A vaccinated child runs a polio fever while playing with an unvaccinated child, and the second child catches the fever, and is de facto inoculated. The incidentally protected herd might be at less risk of contracting the full disease than are those children whose vaccination protects the herd. The Sabin vaccine was the vaccine of choice against polio in the United States after 1962.

There was an alternative to vaccination with live polio virus: vaccination with killed virus, as in the Salk vaccine. And there was a serious cost to using the live instead of the killed vaccine. From the live vaccine some of those vaccinated contracted serious cases of paralytic polio: five to ten cases a year in the United States, or one case per 560,000 first doses of the vaccine (Roberts 1988). From the killed vaccine no one contracts polio. A defense of the general use of the Sabin vaccine was that it offered some herd immunity. (The truth may have been that one set of interests won out against another, because there were great profits to be made from supplying the vaccine.) That is a strange defense. It says that we will put some children at extra risk despite their participation in the vaccination program in order to use them as inoculators of those who have not participated in the program. This strange argument was not given as a public rationale to the parent whose child faced the risks of the Sabin vaccine, and one suspects that many parents would, if given a choice, have chosen the killed Salk vaccine for their children.

Suppose we actually have very good statistics on the alternatives and that it is true that using Sabin live vaccine leads to fewer cases of severe polio than does using Salk killed vaccine. Indeed, suppose it makes a very large difference. Against the policy of using the Sabin vaccine is the principle that we not use some people for the benefit of others—or, in Kantian jargon, we should not use someone as a means only. We seemingly cannot invoke the principle of insufficient reason here to say that it is not possible to say who would benefit and who would suffer costs on their behalf because we know very clearly that those who honorably submit to vaccination suffer expected costs and those who do not submit gain expected benefits. But perhaps we could invoke it in the following way. We cannot know which children have parents who will protect them and which children will not.[7] Hence, deciding in advance to protect all children as well as possible commends the use of Sabin vaccine.

Have we entirely escaped the injunction not to use some to benefit others? The answer to this question turns on our understanding of the relationship of stochastic knowledge to simpler, non-probabilistic knowledge. Many contemporary Kantians insist that stochastic reasoning in certain contexts is no savior, because it is still true that someone, whether identifiable or not, is de facto used as a means. Perhaps getting off the Kantian hook by recourse to the principle of insufficient reason is sophistry. But it is very hard to see, finally, how the policy maker's choice here is other than choosing the program that has best effects overall in the sense of reducing the number of polio victims.

Virtually all policies on large-scale stochastic problems require the imposition of risks on someone. Suppose that a large fraction of our population refused to seek vaccination against smallpox (or polio, AIDS, or whatever) on the claim that they would rather take their chances with nature than with the vaccine, even if nature's dice seem to be more heavily loaded against them. If eradication of the disease depends on eliminating it from human carriers, as eradication of smallpox did and as eradication of AIDS might, leaving this fraction out of our net might mean the continuation of the disease through this generation rather than its final eradication. If we force vaccination on these objectors, as we commonly have done for at least schoolchildren, we force a particular stochastic risk on them in the cause of reducing overall risks.

In the smallpox eradication program discussed below, the World Health Organization (WHO) imposed smallpox vaccination on Third World communities, especially rural communities, with impunity. There was little concern with the violation of anyone's rights—the goal of eliminating smallpox was taken to trump any other consideration. Just because there are massive externalities from anyone's refusal to be protected, it is plausible in such cases to think rights are severely compromised. If I wish to refuse vaccination, then I must live in an inaccessible cave somewhere so that I do not put others at risk.

The form that risks might take can vary enormously for policies on various stochastic problems. For the vaccination policy, the stochastic form of the risk is that, with virtual certainty, it would be distributed across a very small fraction of the affected people. That is to say, it would imply a high cost for a small number of unidentified people. In stark contrast, for the policy of nuclear deterrence, the risk is supposed by strong supporters of deterrence to be a small likelihood of an extraordinarily large cost. For the vaccination policy, we might be quite confident of and in agreement on the numbers who would be affected by alternative policies. For the deterrence policy, we might have only vague guesses about relative numbers affected ex ante and we might substantially disagree on these guesses. Indeed, guesses in print disagree wildly. Such differences in the form and confidence levels of the risks may be very important differences, but they do not have immediately evident moral significance.

Typical of both the vaccination and the nuclear deterrence policies is that they are inherently consequentialist in their rationales. It seems unlikely that we can give a compelling nonconsequentialist rationale for imposing vaccination on objectors. The consequentialist rationale is one of trading off risks to the well-being of some against risks to the well-being of others. For example, in the vaccination case we accept immediate harm to a few in return for reducing harm in the long run to very many. In some nonconsequentialist theories, such as theories of rights, the basic moral principles concern what harms we may inflict on persons. It would typically be wrong on such a theory to kill certain people in order to secure the survival of others, even very many others. But surely, even on such a theory, it cannot be wrong for me to undertake any action whatever that might entail the risk, however slight, of harm or death to another. Consider a trivial example. I often drive my car to a restaurant merely for the sake of a pleasing dinner with friends or family. In doing such a trivial thing, I plausibly risk killing someone in an accident. Even though it would be wrong for me to kill someone in order to have a pleasant dinner—even the best of dinners—it seems incredible to suppose that it is wrong to drive to dinner at the very slight risk of killing someone. This is, in essence, an individual-level analog of large-scale stochastic policies.

Many deontologists seem to have an immediate intuition that it would be wrong to risk doing what it would be wrong to do deliberately (e.g., Donaldson 1985). But such an intuition cannot withstand scrutiny. Individual risks of doing harm to others in order to benefit oneself are inherent in living, and the harms to others that one risks are typically harms that one could not do deliberately without the justification of offsetting benefits. Of course, this is true not only at the individual level but also at the level of social policy. For example, to have a criminal justice system imposes the risk of convicting innocents. We may attempt to reduce that risk but we cannot eliminate it entirely if we have a practical justice system. Despite that risk, we will want such a system, and we will think it more just to have such a system with its particular injustices than not to have one at all. The commonplace claim of deontologists that we cannot trade off harming an innocent in order to achieve some other good is simply belied by any and every system of justice ever contrived. We do it all the time, and almost all of us must admit that we would rather do that than live without a justice system. The overwhelming facts of our actual behavior in this context do not, however, seem to stop deontologists from saying it is impermissible knowingly to act this way.

"If these ideas are right," Judith Jarvis Thomson (1986, 185) says of a similar account of individual actions for minor gain that put others at slight risk of great harm, "—and it really does seem that they are—then risk-imposition does generate an independent problem for moral theory. For there is a further question that then arises, beyond the question what harms we may or may not cause in what circumstances, namely, the question what risks of what harms we may or may not impose in what circumstances."

Thomson's point here, that risk-imposition is a special problem for moral theory, is compelling for a moral theory that focuses on act-kinds, as in many theories that focus on the rightness of actions such as lying, truth telling, killing, or letting die (Thomson 1986, 183). Her point is not necessarily compelling for a theory that focuses on consequences. In a consequentialist theory, the risk of a particular harm may simply carry less weight (discounted to the scale of the risk) than the harm itself—it hardly poses an "independent problem." In a theory of the rightness of act-kinds, however, we must include the probabilities of various outcomes from the acts of various kinds in the definition of the act-kinds if relevant risks are to count. If we do that, the theory begins to smack of consequentialism. If it is characteristic of the theory not to be consequentialist but to value something about acts or persons other than their consequences, this move is apt to seem demoralizing. For such a theory, risk-imposition may be not only a special but also a pernicious problem. If so, the theory is crippled for use in our time, when seemingly every significant action entails risks of harms to others. For this and other reasons, especially the problem of strategic interaction in producing good results, basing moral theory on some notion of a "kind" of action verges on incoherence (see further Hardin 1988, 68–70).

During the years of the nuclear deterrent system, deontological philosophers argued against the deterrence policy of the United States that it violated deontological principles because it threatened the risk of *action* that would have been immoral if deliberately undertaken.[8] Here, the nature of the action is a bit odd. The nuclear weapons of the deterrence system were set up and managed in such a way as to make it almost certain that they would be fired under circumstances of an attack. There need be no central decision maker deciding to use the weapons. Indeed, the deterrent value of the weapons would have been greatest it their use could have been made virtually certain by programming them to go off under certain circumstances. Hence, action was not central to the idea of nuclear deterrence. An action-based moral theory that gives rules for action therefore is irrelevant to criticism of the policy at its most refined.

It was inherent in the institutional structure of the system that if it was to accomplish deterrence (in which case it would never actually be necessary to fire any of the weapons), use of the weapons in relevant circumstances had to be credible. That means that the focus of most deontological criticism of the system was misplaced. The issue was not whether someone must violate a deontological principle by firing the weapons. It was whether an institutional system for making the deterrent force credible was moral. However, deontologists have not typically addressed the issue this way. The focus of any criticism must be on the overall policy, not on any action under that policy that was consistent with the policy. The policy was to prevent war. Perhaps the policy was misdesigned and therefore wrong (even strong defenders of the policy must grant that this is an open question). But the policy of preventing war was not wrong (see further Hardin 1986a). Indeed, it was quite similar in kind to the deterrent criminal justice system which actually does misfire with great regularity. In these days of renewed capital punishment in the United States, we can be stochastically quite sure than many innocents have been executed.

The structural parallel between smallpox eradication and nuclear deterrence is striking. Each was designed to accomplish a very good outcome at the risk of leading to a disastrous outcome. There is a difference. Nature gets to do the massive harm in the smallpox case, although nature is most likely to act through terrorist actions, while a human system does it in the nuclear deterrence case. Among some Catholic moral theorists, this difference is taken to be morally very important. According to the doctrine of double effect, our intentions in the smallpox case were entirely benign and the disastrous outcome, while perhaps fully foreseen, does not count among our intentions. Our intentions in the nuclear deterrence case are to do harm under certain circumstances or, more plausibly in fact, to set up a system that will bring about harm, although one might as soon say we set up the state of affairs in which the grotesque epidemic could happen too, in part merely by failing to continue vaccination and revaccination to keep people immune.

The doctrine of double effect has two roles. First it allows for apportioning moral blame, which may seem important in a religious morality in which, at the end of life, punishment threatens. It introduces a moral version of mens rea to determine culpability as a function of intention rather than effect. The second role of the doctrine is to deal with the complexity of action, which is inherently interaction, as is clear in the policy of nuclear deterrence. Medieval Catholic theorists could already see the implausibility of defining action completely independently of its effects. The doctrine of double effect is, like the early solution to the misfit of Ptolemaic astronomy to the data on planetary movements, an epicycle on the usual cycle. The usual cycle describes simple act-kinds. The epicycle takes effects of actions into account to somehow re-value the actions without quite admitting that they are no longer being treated as act-kinds.

The doctrine has no role in any other plausible context than the religious one of apportioning blame and the rationalizing one of attempting to hold on to the fundamental theory of act-kinds in the face of a far more complex reality. Oddly, invocation of such a doctrine in the religious context implies that god's view of rightness is of the rightness of act-kinds. This is a god who has failed to grasp that, for humans, to act is generally to interact, perhaps because this god seldom has to face problems of interaction but has only known actions analogous to flipping a switch and making light. At least intellectually, despite the undue complexity of the device, the invention of the doctrine of double effect suggests a growing understanding of the nature of the lives we must lead in a real world. The doctrine is a bad response to that understanding because it does not jettison the prior, wrong vision and start anew with a better vision, as eventually was done with astronomy. Instead, it muddles understanding by insisting on the prior vision of simple act-kinds with the rationalized addendum to take other complexities into partial account.

Finally, Thomson's vision of act-kinds is also wrecked by actions that are in essence choices of strategies rather than of outcomes. The very idea of an action in this context (virtually all interactive contexts) loses coherence. A moral theory that is wholly about act-kinds is radically indeterminate because so many of the actions at issue in our lives are interactions.

Institutional Decisions

It is characteristic of stochastic problems of large scale that policies to deal with them are implemented by large, complex organizations, indeed, typically by a complex array of such organizations that themselves behave stochastically. Hence, in understanding how they are implemented, we must understand how relevant institutions can work and are likely to work. This means, inherently, that in deciding what the policies should be we must similarly understand what the possibilities are for implementation. This is merely an instance of the moral philosopher's dictum that "ought" implies "can." If I cannot possibly do something, say, rescue you from a shark, then it is wrong to say that I ought to and it would be wrong to hold me responsible for "failing" to. For example, when the World Health Organization set about the task of eradicating smallpox from the world through its Intensified Smallpox Eradication Program in 1967, it was essentially enabled even to think of that goal as a policy goal by the fact that many nations had already effectively blocked the entry of smallpox into their populations. Hence, WHO could target the few populations in which smallpox was residual and in which it may still have resulted in two million deaths each year (Fenner 1984, 843).

Even then, WHO could only do this as well as it was permitted by its organizational capacities for gaining relevant information on the whereabouts of smallpox, capacities that mainly turned on the ability of certain impoverished nations to discover such information about their own populations. In the United States, a new smallpox case would most likely have become known to national health authorities almost instantly through well-organized channels for reporting. The reporting system is backed by strong sanctions and positive incentives, by communication systems that make such reporting easy and effective, and by a long and well-established tradition of reporting. Such systems were not available to WHO in Ethiopia, Somalia, West Africa, Brazil, and Bangladesh. Its task was simultaneously to vaccinate in all communities in which smallpox was known to be endemic and to try to develop a reporting system that would alert it to additional communities it must vaccinate.

The policy developed by D. A. Henderson and his associates in the WHO program was invented more or less on the fly in the field in order to be efficient and quick. The policy was "case-finding and ring vaccination," or isolation of any affected person and vaccination targeted to those who were especially likely to be exposed—those in a small geographical ring around the victim. If it could be made to work, this policy was more beneficial and less harmful than attempting total immunization of everyone, because it could be done much more efficiently than a full-scale general vaccination. The general vaccination could not as successfully be imposed on everyone as the small-scale ring program could be for the relevant, much smaller community.

To be confident it had succeeded in eradicating the disease (by isolating the last infected person in the world until that person was no longer contagious while also vaccinating everyone in that person's near vicinity), WHO had eventually to develop a nearly complete reporting or discovery system to be sure that all communities everywhere were free of smallpox. Making a mistake of omission might have meant a devastating epidemic. The last case of the more deadly form of smallpox, *Variola major*, in the wild was in Bangladesh in 1975 in a three-year old girl, Rahima Banu. She survived but her further fate is unknown. The last case of *Variola minor* was in Somalia in 1977, in a cook, Ali Maow Maalin, who also survived (Preston 1999, 53). With those two cases, *Variola* in the wild died. After more than two decades, it is inconceivable that it still lives in the wild. It is in the nature of the problem of eradication under the ring vaccination policy that the last cases could, with relative certainty, be known and identifiable—at least after enough time had passed. Indeed, they could become poster celebrities, especially given that they survived to smile about their travails.

Now move ahead a generation and suppose we (at WHO) have decided to go about eradicating polio. We are to some degree in the position of Zabdiel Boylston. We will cause harm to some who would have escaped it otherwise, but we will have reduced the overall incidence of harm from polio. When we now inoculate a particular person in the Sahel or in Bangladesh, it would be odd to suppose we were responsible only for what happens to that person as a result. We cannot divide the vaccination policy into a right and a wrong part, the part that benefits most people and the part that harms a few. These "parts" are one and inseparable. The good is produced at the cost of the harm. *Our responsibility is for the overall policy, given that we understand how it is to be implemented, not merely for isolated results of the implementation of it.* If we send fifty vaccinators into the field and one of these has a polio case result from her vaccinations, we would not wish to say she was responsible for that crippling and maybe fatal illness and that the other vaccinators were responsible only for protections they successfully gave to their vaccinees. It would be utterly silly to say that our unfortunate vaccinator acted immorally in her one case in which the vaccine went awry. We who adopted the policy are essentially responsible for its overall result, including the one death and the presumed thousands of those protected who would otherwise have been afflicted with polio.

This is the essential structure of the form of implementation of policies on major stochastic problems and of the form of moral responsibility for their results. It seems reasonable to say that there is no moral responsibility for the occasional harm from vaccination if the risk of that harm is justified by the great overall benefit from it. Indeed, it is reasonable to say that we may legally coerce people to accept vaccination in some circumstances. For example, in the United States children are required to get certain vaccinations before they are allowed to attend school—but they are also required to attend school, or have been at least until the recent rise of home schooling. Alternatively, we might wish to suppose, as many parents of American children harmed by DPT (diphtheria, pertussis, and tetanus) vaccination have supposed, that we are responsible for the harm to the occasional unfortunate victim of our vaccination (Sun 1985). (It is more reasonable to suppose that we should make it part of our vaccination policy, whose purpose is to enhance the general welfare, to compensate the losers from that policy in some degree just because this addition to our policy further enhances the general welfare both ex ante and ex post.)

A utilitarian naturally would argue that the harms are a trade-off that we suffer in order to avoid even greater harms and that they, while still harms, are not subject to moral criticism if the overall trade-off is justified. Proponents of many other moral theories strongly object to such trade-offs *between people* in many contexts and might similarly object to them in this context. They argue, for example, that individuals or individual rights are inviolable in that, in some sense, they cannot be sacrificed merely in order to make others better off, as was deliberately done in the choice of Sabin rather than Salk vaccine for polio.

Sometimes, theorists who are otherwise hostile to making trade-offs between people allow trade-offs of harms to avoid greater harms. Without such a caveat, an in-principle objection to any trade-offs between individuals is apt to strike almost everyone except arcane moral theorists as odd or even perverse, since it would inherently put us in a moral quandary in the face of many, perhaps all, stochastic policy problems. Imagine the incredulous response of most parents to the moral theorist who insists that children have a right not to be vaccinated if they merely wish not to be, or if their parents wish them not to be. In the world of major policies we must assume that whatever moral principles we follow otherwise, such trade-offs are permissible at least in principle in many cases when lesser likelihood of harm to some is traded for greater likelihood of harm for others. Such trade-offs are the central rationale for many policies. To refuse such trade-offs in principle is to say that even a policy of vaccination with known vaccines, all of which occasionally cause harmful, even deadly, side effects, is impermissible no matter how beneficial those vaccines might be on balance. Often, as will be argued in chapter 8, we could make the claim that everyone benefits ex ante from adopting the policy that entails trade-offs.

Public Policy

Virtually all stochastic problems that provoke major public policy action may involve external effects, both from the behavior being regulated and from the regulation itself. Hence, discussion of risk or probabilities pure and simple, as in individual gambling decisions, misses something at the core of stochastic policy issues. For large-scale stochastic problems it is often inescapably true that the policies will similarly be stochastic. There will be harms as well as benefits resulting from *any* policies that deal with them. Moreover, in some meaningful sense, those harmed may not be those benefited.

There are at least three important characteristics of major policy issues in general that may give rule-based moral theories difficulties. First, such issues can generally be handled only by institutional intervention; they commonly cannot be resolved through uncoordinated individual action. Theories formulated at the individual level must therefore be recast to handle institutional actions and possibilities, as discussed immediately above. Second, major policy issues typically have complicating strategic interactions between individuals at their bases.[9] Third, they commonly are inherently stochastic, as discussed throughout this chapter.

Other issues that are similarly stochastic are policies on the building of highways and various safety devices for them, policies on permitting various levels of air traffic, policies creating long holiday weekends, policies for testing new products, perhaps especially chemical products, policies on the generation of energy, policies on genetic manipulations, and, of course, policies on testing nuclear weapons. Perhaps somewhat less evidently a stochastic problem in large part was the policy of nuclear deterrence. Even the policy of raising the level of education might be associated with a rise in the suicide rate, as Philippa Foot ([1967] 1978, 19) supposes. For the smallpox vaccination, we might be quite confident of just what the odds are, as we may also be for variant policies on highway driving speed, variant levels of taxation on cigarettes or alcohol, and many other policies. For nuclear deterrence before Mikhail Gorbachev unilaterally called off the Cold War while Western leaders such as George Bush insisted that the move was a ruse, we could do little more than guess what would be the likely casualty levels of maintaining or abandoning the deterrence policy.

For many stochastic problems, we can perform tests; for others we cannot. For many we can observe statistical regularities at some microlevel over a long period of time (as in our knowledge of various effects on highway traffic fatalities); for others we can observe them only at a macrolevel at which the learning comes too late to have a beneficial effect on policy (as in nuclear deterrence policy or policies on various contributions to the greenhouse effect, which itself might even turn out to be partially beneficial if it delays a new ice age).

All of these issues have in common their stochastic quality. One might say, "It's wrong for people to die in traffic accidents." But if asked to unpack such a claim, one must grant that its meaning at the policy level can only be that we should suffer certain costs to reduce the incidence of traffic accidents. It cannot imply an absolute injunction against driving. Similarly, in the vaccination case we have two choices: to vaccinate or not to vaccinate even though our vaccine may bring immediate harms. We cannot wait for a perfectly safe vaccine without seeing a high incidence of smallpox or other disease in the meantime. In every case, the policy decision is one between different evils, as in fewer versus more deaths. Waddington ([1960] 1967) supposes that such stochastic problems are the common product of technological innovations. Since we often want the benefits of such innovations, we might have a public policy of indemnifying or especially caring for those who turn out to be the losers from our interventions, although in the United States we traditionally have not done this. The losers on the highways, in vaccination programs, in the airlanes, and in many other contexts have more often borne their own losses, sometimes through ex ante insurance or implicit self-insurance, even though it would seem to be meaningful to say that they have paid to some extent in order to relieve others of various burdens.

In all of these stochastic problems, arguments for and against various policies are often essentially utilitarian. Fewer people will suffer if we vaccinate than if we do not vaccinate. Arguments against deliberate interventions that directly require certain behaviors by people, however, often take the form of defense of libertarian rights. The individual has a right to refuse to be vaccinated or to wear seatbelts or safety helmets. Such arguments virtually never arise in certain contexts, such as air safety, in which my refusal to follow some safety rule may have clear external effects on the safety of others.

The simplest version of the vaccination case has one uniquely interesting quality that distinguishes it from many of these cases. In it, ex ante, or before the policy is implemented, everyone is in the same position. That is to say, the ex ante costs and the ex ante benefits are the same for all. Moreover, the costs are borne almost entirely internally by the affected group. These characteristics are virtually in the nature of the problem. There are minor costs of time and money that may be borne unequally, but these are trivial in comparison to the other costs and benefits. Only free riders on the vaccination of others benefit from significantly unequal costs. The costs of reducing highway traffic fatalities need not be borne entirely internally by the affected group, and the costs and the expected benefits may not be at all equally distributed ex ante. The costs and benefits may be approximately fitted—for example, through carefully designed user fees—to the affected group, but in principle they need not be. Many other major stochastic policy problems are more nearly like the highway traffic problem in this respect than like the vaccination problem. Resolutions of these problems do not naturally entail particular forms of cost sharing.

Concluding Remarks

In a simpler era, the focus on actions and act-kinds might have made approximate sense. Today it does not. Consider the changes that have occurred from the time of Bodo to our time. Bodo was a townsman in the eleventh century in the community around the church of St. Germain des Pres, which in his time was outside Paris (Leijonhufvud 1995). During his lifetime, he may have known a total of about eighty people. All his consumptions came exclusively from his own family's efforts and from his dealings with these eighty people, unless he consumed salt, which would have passed through many hands on its way from the sea, or spices, which would have passed through an even longer chain on their way from Asia to France. We might characterize his life as a relatively limited range of kinds of actions, and we might readily suppose that his morality could be defined in terms of these actions.

Bodo's kind of life is hardly conceivable to the residents of today's Paris, which has long since grown over Bodo's world. In that world, the idea of distributive justice might never have arisen, but a limited, communal principle of charity might have governed as almost a law (see further Hardin 1999c). It has been an extraordinary intellectual achievement for Rawls to argue from a Kantian ethics of actions (that might have fit Bodo's world) to a theory of distributive justice (that might fit ours). He virtually leapt over eight centuries of social development in a few phrases. We will consider whether he landed on his feet in the next chapter.

The difference between Bodo's and our world is not merely in Waddington's changed technology. It is also in the richer range of activities in which we engage. Unless action theory can be substantially remade for our time, much of deontology should be relegated to the history of thought, particularly to an era of history when action theory was grossly misconceived but in which the misconceptions left it still approximately suited to the times, as in Bodo's time, many centuries past. Kant's action theory had already ceased to make sense long before his time.

In closing, I should note that there is not a rational choice or pragmatic equivalent of moral rules. Moral rules have the role of trumping a richer range of considerations only in certain moral theories. Rules of thumb and teaching the young rules of honesty, sociability, and reliability are pragmatic rules for psychological reasons, not for reasons of handling indeterminacy that would swamp the range of choice. They are always pragmatically up for revision or rejection. To follow a pragmatic deontology would make no sense. Rules are an odd response to indeterminacy because they must be radically incomplete. And some sets of moral rules, such as Kantian rules, fail almost entirely to be action-guiding in some contexts that any moral theory must take seriously, such as policy contexts.

Some have argued for moral rules more or less on analogy with law. Law is, of course, in large part a set of rules (Hart 1961). Law is also inherently incomplete and it should be. It should not cover all behavior and it cannot be made to work well in covering behavior for which there are natural epistemological limits on institutions (see further Hardin 1994). It must also be adaptable to changing conditions and understandings. This means that there must be an institutional structure in place to revise laws. There is no such structure for overseeing and revising moral rules unless, perhaps, there is a religious body with such power, as in Catholic medieval Europe or in much of the Islamic world today. This solution to the indeterminacy of moral rules, however, is a matter of historical accident that some religious body has achieved coercive power, generally to the detriment rather than the benefit of a populace.

It is not my purpose here to discuss moral theory per se. The point of the discussion has been to focus on rules as a device for simplifying the world by ignoring its indeterminacies. That move is a device of moralists and not of others. Unlike moral rules, pragmatic rules are always subject to revision in the face of experience, and they can always be trumped by weightier considerations. There is a sense in which they can be tested just as scientific causal claims can be tested. Moral rules all too often descend from metaphysical or transcendental reason, from religious proclamation (by the lucky coteries of those with a direct line to some god), or from bald intuitions. Although some moral rules might be subject to revision from, say, better transcendental argument, they are not readily subject to scientific testing but are, rather, "above" being sullied by such testing.

If one were to take up moral theories in general, it should be evident that several other moral theories must also have difficulties with stochastic issues. For example, virtue theories are largely inadequate to the task of handling major policy problems. Virtue theories often put ends and means in a functional relationship, so that to specify what is a virtue, we must first say what is the end we wish the virtuous to achieve. Thereafter, a person is virtuous (good) to the extent she has the relevant characteristics. If narrowing our concern to acts sweeps much of the moral world under a rug, concern with character virtually hides most of that world from us. This is to handle stochastic problems by denying their significance.

Consent and contract theories might in principle be able to handle stochastic problems, but they can do so only at a rationalist level of hypothetical consent, and even at that level moral theorists seem unable to reach consensus. Theories that are based in the autonomy or rights of persons are arguably far more interesting for the evaluation of policies. Yet bald rights theories turn to non-sense in the face of such disasters as a disease such as smallpox, with all its external effects of individual actions. Autonomy theories are acutely afflicted with problems of stochastic processes, and it is to the Kantian branch of such theories that most of the discussion here has been addressed.

Finally, note that the central, most fundamentally objectionable aspect of Kantian *theory* is the following two steps: first, to deduce what principle one would want everyone to follow in an ideal world, the Kingdom of Ends, in which everyone is an end and a rational agent in a fairly strenuous sense; second, then to insist that one should follow that principle in our ordinary world, which is full of agents who are not rational in Kant's exacting sense, who are often sleazy, venal, and vicious. Virtually everyone can agree that the so-called Generalization Argument (What if everyone did that?), which says that one should behave as one would want to be able to generalize for everyone to behave, is specious just because, in essence, that principle is argued directly for our actual world, in which it does not make sense because it has perverse implications (see Hardin 1988, 65–68). Yet it is no more specious than Kant's entire deduction.

Kant's ideal world of the Kingdom of Ends is inordinately benign and simple. In it everything is virtually sure to be good. In such a world, action is inherently simplistic, so simplistic as to allow us to think it analogous to flipping light switches to achieve good effects immediately from our action. That world bears little relation to the complex world in which we have to live, in which, because of strategic interactions and stochastic problems, action is radically more complexly related to outcomes. Any inference from Kant's transcendental vision that Schindler must be morally worse for his lying (doing wrong formally, though not materially) to Nazi officials than he would have been for letting many people die is heinous and stupid. Schindler's actions were among the morally most praiseworthy that we have ever known. The fundamental problem of the theory that makes his actions wrong is that it ignores the nature of our world, in which action is inherently interaction with others; it is therefore more complex than action in any theory that counts some actions as definitively good and others as definitively bad merely on the basis of the kinds of action they are. In an indeterminate or stochastic world it makes no sense to conceive actions the way Kant seemingly does, as something it would always be right or always wrong to do. Schindler's actions can only with undue complexity be called act-kinds. His actions took many forms, many of them involving deceit and lies of various kinds, but they were generally motivated by a single purpose: to save lives by rescuing people from consignment to Nazi death camps.

A system of deontological rules might be appropriate for teaching children how to act in ways that are, in fact, likely to be in their interest, or for teaching the intellectually impaired, as Mill argued from his somewhat elitist stance. It might also have worked well enough in Bodo's extremely simple world. Finally, it might be fit for an autocratic and powerful religious body that rules more or less ex cathedra. But in our adult world, it misses almost everything of significance. It misses so much because it miss-defines actions by individuals in society as act-kinds rather than as the interactions that they typically are. In this case, hiding the indeterminacy that characterizes our world harms the chance we have of living well in that world and the chance we have of doing well by others.

Chapter Seven

Indeterminate Justice

APART FROM LAW and economics, the most influential area in contemporary political philosophy is the debate over distributive justice that has been sparked by John Rawls (1999 [1971]).[1] Any effort to define a principle of distributive justice that would deal with the demanding range of its issues seems likely to be rent with problems of indeterminacy. In the most sophisticated such effort to date, Rawls's attempt to master the complexities at issue suggests how difficult it is to handle the indeterminacies. This should probably not come as a surprise, because the indeterminacy of mere interests seems likely only to be confounded if we add issues of collective valuation, as a theory of distributive justice must do in some way. If individual-level rational choice and the general array of social interactions are all subject to indeterminacy, such principles as distributive justice are almost certain to be indeterminate.

Rawls himself sees this issue clearly. Although this presumably is not how he would characterize his effort, a large part of the hundreds of pages Rawls has written is dedicated to simplifying the issues in ways that allow more nearly determinate conclusions, as he asserts (56, 65 [65, 75]). In the end, although we cannot agree that his theory is determinate, still we may conclude that some of his tricks succeed in narrowing the focus of what is at stake in distributive justice. (We know too much, however, to expect Rawls to narrow that focus as sharply as Hobbes did. Hobbes assumed gross social-scientific ignorance that could not even allow a judgment whether democracy or autocracy is the form of government that would serve us best.) Among theorists discussed in this book, he is among the most forthright in recognizing the deep problems of indeterminacy that he faces and among the most ingenious in trying to overcome them. Yet his theory is finally indeterminate, perhaps grievously so. It is instructive to see why this is true. Most conspicuously, some of the indeterminacy has been swept under the rug of his category of primary goods, as will be argued later.

The value of considering this theory here is that, apart from utilitarianism, it is the only contemporary normative theory at the societal level that has been broadly articulated and debated and that has been diligently designed to try to fit it to the world by someone who consciously wants it to be determinate. It is therefore instructive to see how indeterminacies still afflict it. My purpose is not to expound or criticize the theory overall but only to address its problems with indeterminacy. In a world that is inherently indeterminate, a suitable theory of distributive justice must perhaps itself be indeterminate, and its indeterminacies must accommodate those of the world where relevant. Hence, the mere fact of indeterminacies does not disqualify Rawls's theory, although the specific character of these might disqualify it by making it incoherent.

Rawls begins with the apparent conflict between equality and efficiency, two orthogonal values. The efficiency that concerns him is productive efficiency. That is to say, he is concerned with Hobbesian productive efficiency, not Paretian static efficiency. (The latter is strictly about efficiency of bilateral trades to redistribute what goods we already have through market exchange. It is static because it involves no production.)[2] Hence, in Rawls's account equality is about allocation, and efficiency is about production of what is to be allocated. His theory of justice is an effort to package these two considerations into a single decision rule. At the collective level, we want equality; at the individual level each of us wants prosperity. Rawls wants to put our resources and incentives into producing the largest possible set of relevant goods for distribution in order to get prosperity. Conflict with equality arises if individual productivity depends heavily on incentives, as it will if the way to induce greater production is to let effective producers have larger-than-average shares of the society's wealth, income, or consumption. Hence, the concern with productive efficiency already suggests the likelihood of indeterminacy in the trade-off between production and allocation of goods.

Rawls offers a way to bridge the apparent conflict. To make this work, he attempts to do something roughly like what Hobbes and Coase do. He narrows the range of possible efficient outcomes that we need consider. In his contractarian account of the creation of a sovereign, Hobbes fell back on epistemological ignorance to reduce the set; and in his argument against overturning an extant government, he far too confidently asserted a social-science claim that even a little bit of opposition to a regime threatened devastating civil war. Coase uses market values to trade beyond the production that would come from the bare allocations of the property rights assignments. Rawls uses his difference principle (65–68 [76–79]; Rawls 1996, 6–7), which requires that all inequalities—political and economic—"are to the greatest benefit of the least advantaged members of society." Rawls's focus is that of Hobbes on the general structure of political-legal order, and not that of Coase on the resolution of marginal interactions against the background of an established political-legal order. Rawls is concerned to construct government ex ante, even ex nihilo.

Part of the great appeal of Rawls's theory for moral theorists is that it combines the two major streams of thought, one based on egalitarianism and one based on mutual advantage (see, e.g., 13, 66 [13, 76–77]), that are probably the dominant visions of modern political philosophy (Barry 1989).[3] Egalitarianism has ready populist appeal although, surprisingly, it may have had no articulate advocate with a substantially worked out theory before Rawls. Mutual advantage is essentially the distributive justice of the Scottish Enlightenment philosophers David Hume and Adam Smith, and it is the core of ordinal utilitarianism (Hardin 1988).[4] Indeed, it can reasonably be characterized as the theory of justice of Hobbes as well, although Hobbes might blanch at the meaning *justice* has taken on in normative political philosophy in intervening centuries. Mutual advantage has a long history of articulate argument in its defense while, strangely, egalitarianism hardly has any, perhaps because its supporters have taken its value or goodness for granted.

In very brief summary, the theory of justice as fairness has four main elements: the set of basic or primary goods, equality, mutual advantage, and, to regulate the combination of these two, the difference principle. Rawls's solution to the problem of combining equality and efficiency—the economist's big trade-off—is to resort to a particular claim of fairness. What a society produces is largely a result of the way that society is organized; it is not merely the sum of what all individuals would do entirely on their own without social organization of their efforts. Because the total product is determined socially, the reward to individuals for the social product should therefore be determined socially. Rawls supposes that a determination that any rational person would accept ex ante is to allow all inequalities that produce better lives for those who are worst off. If a system that allows some very few to be billionaires produces enough to raise the well-being of the worst-off class to a higher level than any other system would, then the apparent inegalitarianism is fair.

Well-being and *welfare* are inadequate terms to capture what Rawls wishes to equalize. Among his primary goods, he includes certain political rights, a very vague concern with respect, and standard welfare concerns. He treats all of these as resources or enablers rather than as welfare. In particular, they are resources for a citizen to have a political role in the society. Unfortunately, his cluster of concerns seems to have several dimensions, and it is not easy to define a notion of equality to cover all these dimensions, as though they could simply be added up. Rawls's fairness is therefore murky and possibly incoherent. Until I address the nature of the primary goods below, however, in order to focus here on the other elements of the theory, I will assume for the moment that his notion of equality of these primary good resources is a simple one that can be applied straightforwardly.

Rawls's more general concern with the trade-off between equality and efficiency suggests a focus on resources that are the usual goods of a productive society. This is slightly odd, because a large fraction of what is actually produced is consumption goods and services, and it is difficult to conceive these as contributing to resources rather than welfare (recall the discussion of Posner's wealth maximization, in chapter 4). I will discuss this issue further below.

Value pluralists such as Isaiah Berlin (1976; Gray 1996, 38–75), Joel Feinberg (1975), and Thomas Nagel (1977) insist on multidimensionality, so that they essentially insist on indeterminacy and suppose we and our theories should live with it. That is to say, they think there are many different and independent principles or criteria we would want a theory of justice to fit, and that there is no overarching principle for ordering or combining these. Theirs is an eminently plausible position because indeterminacy is at the heart of our social life and arguably of our values. Rawls takes the position of such pluralists seriously in his discussion of intuitionism (30–36 [34–40]), but he supposes that his difference principle handles this particular problem "since it ranks all combinations of objectives according to how well they promote the prospects of the least favored" (280 [318]).

Rawls thus puts two incommensurable values (welfare and egalitarianism) together. In principle, this is probably the cleverest move in all of contemporary political philosophy. He does so by making the theory of justice determinate, at least in the abstract. Indeed, this is his explicit claim: the difference principle "removes the indeterminateness of the principle of efficiency [mutual advantage]" (65 [75]). Earlier, he argues that intuitionists can claim to produce a determinate outcome, but they can do so only by invoking a "rule"—as in Rawls's argument from indifference curves (33 [37])—that is not an objective rule that anyone else could simply follow, as anyone could follow the difference principle. Making his own theory overcome indeterminacy is a central, driving concern that has largely been neglected in the voluminous literature responding to Rawls's theory.

Dimensionality is still an open question for Rawls's theory because he has not worked out articulately how the elements of his political resources fit together (as opposed to how they are allocated), although he supposes his theory is determinate in principle (56, 65 [65, 75]). Anyone who thinks indeterminacy is an extraordinarily difficult problem in social analysis must think this a signal achievement in principle.

I will consider several aspects of justice as fairness as a theory of distributive justice. First I will give a brief account of the nature of the problem of the interaction between productivity and equality, which motivates the theory, then an outline of the elements of the theory of justice as fairness, including a simplified account of its central effort to balance productivity with equality, and then an account of the complexities of mutual advantage. Then I will turn briefly to the relationship between the two-stage argument behind the Coase theorem and that for justice as fairness. Finally I will take up the three related issues of resources, primary goods, and the difference principle. Rawls's primary goods are less simple than merely a single-dimensional resource, and their complexity entails a fundamental indeterminacy in the larger theory.

Equality versus Productive Efficiency

I will assume that it is not necessary to motivate a concern with equality in a theory of (distributive) justice. The problem, rather, is how to achieve it. Rawls recognizes and perhaps accepts the sociological claim of the classical economists that genuine equality can be achieved only by reducing the status of all to some common denominator (see Hume, quoted below; Scitovsky 1952; Okun 1975). The result would be loss of incentive to be very productive, so that the egalitarian society would be generally impoverished. As Hume, F. A. Hayek (1960a, 44), and many others suppose, we might make the poorest better off by letting the able go on to reap far better than equal rewards (see more generally Hardin 1988, 126–37). Rawls accepts this possibility and makes it his principle of mutual advantage.

Hume, writing about 1750, saw distributive justice in the modern egalitarian sense as pernicious. He attributed concern with such an abstract principle as egalitarianism to writers who argued from pure reason with no attention to the possibilities of their actual world and to such religious fanatics as the seventeenth-century Levellers, who wanted to build a Christian, egalitarian, subsistence-farming society in England (Winstanley [1652] 1973). Although Hume may have had a lingering commitment to arguments from merit, his actual statement of the problems with egalitarian distribution could hardly be more modern in its arguments. He wrote that

> ideas of perfect equality . . . are really, at bottom, impracticable; and were they not so, would be extremely *pernicious* to human society. Render possessions ever so equal, men's different degrees of art, care, and industry will immediately break that equality. Or if you check these virtues, you reduce society to the most extreme indigence; and instead of preventing want and beggary in a few, render it unavoidable to the whole community. The most rigorous inquisition too is requisite to watch every inequality on its first appearance; and the most severe jurisdiction, to punish and redress it. But besides, that so much authority must soon degenerate into tyranny, and be exerted with great partialities; who can possibly be possessed of it, in such a situation as here supposed? ([1751] 1975, sec. 3, pt. 2, p. 194)[5]

In this passage, Hume raises two of the standard arguments against equality, which can be stated in contemporary vocabulary as follows. First, equality entails reduced incentives to those who are especially productive and leads to a trade-off between equality and efficiency of production (Scitovsky 1952; Okun 1975). Second, giving a potentially capricious government the power to achieve equality gives it the power to do much else, including very undesirable, tyrannous things. One might add that such a powerful government might make its major office holders essentially wealthy, as happened in many communist and other autocracies, in some of which the office of autocrat has become an inherited right.

Hume canvassed these problems after first granting a view, later developed by F. Y. Edgeworth (1881) and other utilitarians, that with typical inequality, we must "rob the poor of more satisfaction than we add to the rich, and that the slight gratification of a frivolous vanity, in one individual, frequently costs more than bread to many families, and even provinces." He did not imagine the vastness of the fortune of Bill Gates, whose wealth—at this writing, in the tens of billions of dollars—exceeds that of many of the poorest nations in the world taken together. Despite this clear, essentially utilitarian appeal of equality, however, Hume thought it a bad idea because impracticable to achieve.

Let us spell out the central problem in simple terms. Complete equality of income (and wealth, but let us briefly assume away wealth) is tantamount to *making total production a collectively provided good to be shared equally among all the producers*. My contribution to that good makes no difference to me, because, in the United States for example, I would get from my own contribution about one two-hundred-millionth part of what I produce. If per worker income is about $20,000, I will get one-one-hundredth of a penny from my own effort, and the rest of my $20,000 from the efforts of others. This system would entail essentially zero incentive to anyone to work for the sake of income. Some might work for other reasons, such as the pleasures of the work or, as in the theory of the new socialist person, the good of the society. With Rawls (13 [14]), however, we should rule out the likelihood of "strong and lasting benevolent impulses."

Add the complication (a bit of overkill) that a large percentage of all workers in any extant nation probably do not like their jobs and could not be motivated to work very hard by love of the work. Nor is this an aberration of the present organization of economies, as Marxists have sometimes claimed (when there were Marxists). Genuine egalitarianism in small-group anthropological societies can probably be made to work relatively well, but to do so it may often have required massive sanctioning power from the group against genuine shirkers. Norms of exclusion in small groups can be extremely powerful (see further Hardin 1995, chap. 4). But these are not a workable device for a very large society of joint producers, where motivating people would require a universalistic norm of commitment to the larger society. Such a norm is very difficult to sustain (Hardin 1995, chap. 5).

In sum, we cannot expect a purely egalitarian system to work at all. It will not merely be inferior in productivity to a system with inequalities that are used to motivate contributions. It will be destitute. Equality as a goal must therefore be compromised in favor of at least some productivity. A sound compromise would be mutually advantageous to all of us.

Justice as Fairness

It is commonly supposed that so-called theories, as opposed to mere commentaries, on morality must be consistent and complete for the range of their application. In actual fact, no extant theory may meet these demanding conditions fully. Classical additive utilitarianism is, in principle, complete and, because it has only one dimension on which to measure value, it is also internally coherent, although its value theory may not be conceptually coherent.[6] Mutual-advantage theories are also in principle coherent. But because they are sometimes indeterminate, they are not complete. For example, there might be two mutually advantage outcomes, in one of which you are better off and in the other of which I am better off. The simple criterion of mutual advantage cannot say which one we should choose. Arguably, however, the world to which we apply such a theory is best fitted to an indeterminate theory because that world is indeterminate. Hence, the institutions we might design to fit our theory of justice are not fully determined, as is true also for Rawls's institutions (176 [201]).

Because Rawlsian distributive justice is compounded of two apparently incommensurable and even conflicting elements, we might expect it not to cohere. Indeed, the joining of Rawls's different values must logically fail or it must include an independent third principle to balance mutual advantage against equality when they conflict. Again, Rawls adopts a third principle: his difference principle. Under this principle, equality and mutual advantage are combined analytically without any need for balancing them. Under the difference principle, if mutual advantage can apply, then it does, automatically. In rough terms, which will be clarified below, first—or lexicographically—we do equality, insisting on perfect equality. Then, we apply the mutual-advantage principle to this state of equality, starting with the worst-off class (in this case everyone, because all are equal). Perhaps there are many mutual-advantage moves available. We choose that one in which the worst-off class is best off.[7]

In this three-part theory—egalitarianism, mutual advantage, and the difference principle—mutual advantage is just ordinal utilitarianism, and one must suppose it has the indeterminacy problems of ordinal utilitarianism.[8] Justice as fairness does not necessarily have those problems, however, because in it the looseness of mutual advantage is constrained by the lexicographic invocation of equality through the difference principle. Again, the combination of equality and mutual advantage is therefore potentially determinate, at least in principle. Rawls's egalitarianism, however, is a bit messy. It is interpersonally comparable and it is in part cardinal, but it seems likely that it is also in part indeterminate. It is made up of several items—including rights and wealth, a bit of oil and water—that are commonly discussed as resources and that must somehow be compared or otherwise combined. If you have more X and less Y than I have, how do we compare our individual totals of resources? Rawls and some of his followers sometimes assume this problem away, but Rawls sometimes grants it clearly (e.g., Rawls 1996, 180–181n).

There is one other potential flaw in this device. When we are comparing one state of affairs to another and saying that the worst-off class in the first state is better off than the worst-off class in the second state, we need not be comparing the *same* worst-off class in each state. The worst-off class in one state could be one occupational group, while that in another state could be a different occupational group. Hence, the device is exclusively ex ante, because ex ante we are deciding on the fates of unidentified people. We do not apply the mutual advantage criterion to an extant real-world distribution in order to determine whether to move to another distribution. We apply it in principle to all possible states of affairs without regard to the actual population in the worst-off group. We are saved from some problems by a principle of insufficient reason, as Hobbes was. Rawls asserts that principle in his invocation of a veil of ignorance behind which we choose—or one of us chooses—principles for organizing society.

Mutual Advantage

In general, if we are to say that some way of organizing society is mutually advantageous, we must say advantageous with respect to which other way of organizing it. This means that, in effect, a mutual-advantage theory is likely to be almost static, because moving from any actual or presumptive state of affairs to any other is likely to make some worse off even though it might make most people better off. A mutual-advantage theory might therefore be relatively determinate for the simple reason that it would prescribe stasis. Rawls attempts to avoid this debility by stipulating the particular initial state to which any other state is to be compared. The initial state is that in which everyone is equally well off with respect to the limited set of goods in his primary goods.[9] For the time being, let us continue to simplify the category of primary goods and refer to these goods as a resource, of which an individual could command more or less.

The initial state of equal resources might be one in which everyone is very poor, because, as argued above and by Hume, Hayek, and many others, without differential incentives for productivity, the society of equals might be severely unproductive. Those who might be more productive, because they have greater talent or otherwise, might not be motivated to make great effort that redounds almost entirely to the benefit of others. Indeed, *no one* will have incentive to produce things that will primarily benefit others through an egalitarian allocation of what is produced, so that pure equality might mean abject poverty.

Using differential incentives, however, is likely to lead not only to greater productivity but also, of course, to inequality—perhaps massive inequality (Rawls 1996, 281–82; Okun 1975).

Let us restate Rawls's argument in a simple way that separates the incentive effects for production from the egalitarian urge. Much of what we produce can be thought of either as consumption goods or as resources. For the moment, however, let us consider it as merely additions to the resources that are to be divided. We can increase the total mass of resources to be divided by allowing side payments for productivity. If these payments are less than the additional resources that they lead to, then there is a net gain of resources to be divided in the society.[10] If this net gain is equally divided, everyone is therefore better off than in the initial state. But those who are stimulated to be more productive by side payments are now better off than those who receive merely an equal share of the excess production.

We therefore have *two parallel allocation systems*: the allocation of side payments to stimulate productivity and the allocation of equal shares to all from the total pool of production net of the side payments that have been paid. Even those who get only an equal share of the production net of side payments, however, are better off than they would have been in a purely egalitarian system. Hence, it is in the interest of those who are poorest in this system to have the inequalities that lead to their greater prosperity from the system. If we assume that the two allocation systems allocate essentially the same kind of thing, then there is only a causal and not additionally a conceptual problem in relating the two.

Why is taking part of what I produce and distributing it to others fair? Because the rewards we each get from our efforts are largely socially or collectively produced in two ways. First, as Arrow (1978, 278–99) says, "There are significant gains to social interaction above and beyond what individuals and subgroups can achieve on their own. The owners of scarce personal assets do not have substantial private use of these assets; it is only their value in a large system which makes these assets valuable." Others help me produce what I produce; in fairness, they should have a share in its value. The second way rewards are differentially related to the way we organize socially follows from this point. My productivity is not merely the result of my efforts but also of the social arrangements that help to turn my efforts into something more productive than they would be if I produced alone. We choose, according to the difference principle, which way to organize society. We could have organized the society in a way that would have made others better off and me worse off. Therefore, in a strong sense, it is only fair that I should share part of my bounty with others whose contributions are less rewarded just because we live under the present set of arrangements rather than another.

Justice as Fairness and the Coase Theorem

Recall the move of Coase (discussed in chapter 5). He achieves ordinal improvements for both parties through the generation of extra *cardinal* net income that can be shared in a way that makes both parties better off *ordinally* in comparison to their own individual states ex ante in the status quo. An analogous device is used by Rawls. This may sound prima facie implausible, because Rawls's theory of justice shares with Hobbes's theory a concern with the whole structure of governance, whereas Coase's theorem is about how to achieve greater productive efficiency at the margin of a working economic and legal order. Rawls's device is, starting from a state of equality, to introduce unequal rewards that enhance productivity and then to share the extra gains from that activity among all citizens. Mutual advantage is achieved by allocating what is essentially a cardinal resource across all citizens, just as Coase could achieve mutual advantage by allocating cardinal profits in dollars over the relevant parties.

Unfortunately, there is a substantial difference between these two devices that suggests the possible incoherence of Rawls's move. Coase's device is applied in a context in which there is a price system, so that both parties to a Coasean bargain can weigh the costs of their productive efforts against the income from those efforts in extant prices. Moreover, if they reallocate rights to the use of some resource in order to increase productivity, the loser in that reallocation—say, Coase's farmer (discussed in chapter 1)—can assess the costs to herself from that reallocation through the reduced income from her own production. She can then know how much she will have to be compensated in order to make her better off than she would have been without the reallocation of productive resources from her kind of production.

Just as there has to be a going price system to make Coase's move, so too there has to be in place a system that gives measure to the elements in Rawls's bundle of resources. Rawls does not have an extant price system for assessing the useful value of various resources to citizens because his allocation is ex ante before there is even a going economy, when there are no prices. Hence Rawls's resources must be measured in some other way. For example, they might be measured intrinsically. One intrinsic value theory, the labor theory of value (as discussed in chapter 4), will not work because it is contradictory in this context. The chief point of differential incentives is to get those *whose labor is worth more* (because it is more productive) to contribute more to the pool of resources. More generally, we cannot place values on various resources ex ante. They gain their value in a going economic, legal, and social order.[11] The initial sense that it is implausible to suppose Rawls and Coase have analogous theories is, for this reason, correct. Their theories have analogous struc-

Hence, while we might claim substantial coherence for a welfarist concern with resources, we cannot claim much, if any, coherence for a political concern with resources. Welfare is conceptually prior to resources in the former. Is there some vision of political roles that is conceptually prior to political resources? At this point the theory is woefully underelaborated and indeterminate.[13] It is conceptually indeterminate for public-choice, game-theoretic, and other reasons. That is to say, it is *inherently indeterminate*—and not merely fortuitously indeterminate because of the limits of the present level of social scientific understanding. The problem with a theory of political resources is not merely that we lack theory, but that theory is convincingly hostile to the very idea of a determinate theory of resources.

The turn to resourcist theories in our time has partly, perhaps even primarily, been a response to apparent difficulties in welfarist conceptions. Somehow, focusing on resources is supposed to simplify analysis, as focusing on money might. To make resources conceptually independent of welfare, resource theorists treat access to them as a matter of fairness rather than of outcomes. Hence, we are concerned to give everyone an equal opportunity rather than an equal result. After exercising their opportunities, some turn out to be Bill Gates or Warren Buffet and some turn out to be destitute. Some Ph.D.'s in philosophy teach at Harvard and others drive taxis in greater Boston. The turn to opportunity is already the move of Rawls, but in Rawls's discussions the separation of resources from welfare is less clear.

Consider one further issue in the nature of resources. Rawls (1996, 178–87) recurs to resources in part because he wants interpersonal comparability, without which he perhaps supposes that the idea of equality makes little sense. It is not clear what it would mean to say resources are interpersonally comparable in the way Bentham and others might say utility or welfare is interpersonally comparable. But some of the resources included in Rawls's primary goods, as discussed immediately below, are objective rather than subjective. They are also freely tradable in a way that welfare clearly is not. To trivialize this point, I can give you my money but I cannot give you my happiness (but maybe you would take my occasional unhappiness?). They are also often essentially cardinal. If they have all of these characteristics, they are like von Neumann-Morgenstern money-metric utility in games, which looks and behaves very much like money. Rawls's income and wealth fit this characterization. Some of the other elements of his list of primary goods may also be objective rather than subjective, but they do not have the other characteristics here.

PRIMARY GOODS

Very briefly, consider a conspicuous problem in the nature of Rawls's primary goods and arguably in any political theory of distributive justice that is concerned with equality. Here is the list of the primary goods, briefly worded (78–81 [90–95]; 1996, 181).

1. Basic rights and liberties
2. Freedom of movement and free choice of occupation
3. Powers and prerogatives of positions of responsibility in political and economic institutions
4. Income and wealth
5. The social bases of respect. (386–91 [440–46])

Rawls (1996, 179) conceives these as mutually advantageous for all. Hence we must see them as like resources or welfare. Presumably, Rawls would reject a welfarist conception of them, and in his discussions of them, he generally treats them as resources for full political participation in the society.

Whatever our status with respect to the other elements in the list of primary goods, we can increase wealth through differential rewards. Now, does the increased wealth affect any of the other items in the list? Surely it would in the case of such wealth as that of several billionaires in the United States. Perhaps it already does even for someone in the upper-middle class. We therefore need a causal theory of how these items interact as well as a principle for how to weigh them against each other. Suppose my income increases considerably because of the economic boom that also creates the billionaires. Does that increase offset the relative loss in equality of political access I then have as the billionaires gain much greater political influence than most of us have?

No one has given a compelling or clear account of what *respect* in the last item in the list is.[14] One characteristically vague formula is: "to respect another as a moral person is to try to understand his aims and interests from his standpoint and to present him with considerations that enable him to accept the constraints on his conduct" (297 [338]). Moreover, whatever it is, it seemingly must come from other individuals in the society, not merely from the state. We therefore need first to know what it is and second to know how it could be organized or caused by a state. Although it is vague, it sounds good and democrats and egalitarians would presumably be glad to have it. Rawls includes it in his list partly in response to early criticism of his theory, "particularly to its failure to consider the relevance of status" (xix [x]), and partly to handle other issues. Suppose we get the idea well defined and, even more implausibly, we come to have an understanding of how different ways of organizing government impinge on respect. We then must decide how to trade status off against other items in the list (see 55 and 217 [247]). Rawls grants in general that there might be trade-offs among the primary goods, although he also sometimes denies this point (182 [207]).[15] That there must be trade-offs virtually follows from the fact that all of these items can vary independently across individuals depending on how society is politically and economically organized.

Without a principle for weighing or aggregating the elements among the primary goods together, we cannot reach a determinate resolution of whether the difference principle applies. Rawls has acknowledged this point in a footnote.[16] (One is reminded of a Monty Python skit in which a police inspector says to a manufacturer of such candies as "crunchy frog" that inclusion of dead frogs in the candy should not merely be mentioned in the fine print of the list of ingredients. Rather, it should be screamed out in large red letters across the front of the package.) One need only know that there is more than one kind of element among the primary goods to suspect that this must be a problem.

The point of introducing the primary goods was apparently to simplify what we must provide to citizens and to escape the complexities and indeterminacies of welfare. The complexities of welfare arise largely from its subjective nature. Here, however, we encounter complexity from an ostensibly objective set of considerations that, with the exception of income and wealth, may be impossible to measure well enough to rank differences between individuals. To rank differences even for a single individual when two of the items in the list vary in opposite directions may be impossible, especially if we are to rank them objectively, in keeping with the objective appeal of each of the items. The label "primary goods" is a rug under which these indeterminacies have been swept.

THE DIFFERENCE PRINCIPLE

Recall the statement of the difference principle, which requires that all inequalities "are to the greatest benefit of the least advantaged members of society" (Rawls 1996, 6–7). In this statement there is the faint whiff of a dual maximization problem, like that of the incoherent Benthamite formula, "the greatest good of the greatest number," which has been rightly ridiculed, as mentioned briefly in chapter 4. Rawls is fully cognizant of the incoherence of the idea of dual maximization (280–81 [318]). Indeed, he uses that incoherence as an argument in support of his focus—he calls it democratic (65 [75])—on the benefits of the least-advantaged people in the society, as opposed to the maximization of the benefits of all, which cannot coherently be a goal for us. That is to say, a reason for introducing the difference principle is to block any appeal to dual maximization for combining the incommensurable values of welfare and equality. The only way to combine them is through his independent difference principle.

If we suppose that Rawls genuinely avoids dual maximization here, we might then suppose that the issue is merely in the fuzziness of the meaning of the least advantaged. Rawls attempts to escape this problem by speaking of classes of people of varying degrees of prosperity (or whatever one would call having his primary goods at a high level). This introduces extensive indeterminacy in the defining of classes. In the initial idealized state (if one can call the state of abject but equal poverty an ideal) of complete equality, there is one class of people. When we speak of making the worst-off class better off, it is clear who they are: everybody. Beyond this move, however, it is not at all clear what it would mean to speak of a worst-off class.

The term *class* suggests some significant—or at least noticeable—break between the worst-off class and the next-worst-off class. Classes must primarily be defined by levels of resources in many contexts, such as in nations in which all citizens have essentially equal political and economic rights but some own factories in which others merely work for wages. Yet the distribution of people by resource level seems likely to be almost continuously graduated. There will be no obvious break points to say this is the worst-off class, this the next worst off, and so forth. Division of a society into such classes therefore seems almost surely unworkable. It is easy to imagine classes defined by status, as in a feudal or caste system, but not defined by income or wealth in a modern industrial state. Any stipulation of classes in the latter will be arbitrary.

Unfortunately, this is a fundamentally important problem, because the difference principle has the task of overcoming the indeterminacy of combining equality and mutual advantage. Almost the entire brilliance of Rawls's project is to achieve such a combination. The foundations of his move, however, are laid on sand if we cannot define classes meaningfully for the difference principle. Our first task when we start from equality is to pick a state of affairs out of all of those that are mutually advantageous to the state of complete equality (there might be very many). If (because the idea of class is ill defined) we cannot stipulate a second-worst-off class to allow us to narrow this choice set to one or at least a smaller number of states, we face indeterminacy at the beginning of the exercise.

Without a credible difference principle or some alternative device to bridge equality and mutual advantage, we almost certainly have to concede that our theory is massively indeterminate and unable to help us select between alternative social, political, and economic forms and institutions. Egalitarianism alone seems likely to entail destitution in our world—this recognition is essentially the beginning of Rawls's theory. But without a workable difference principle, we have no principle for selecting one mutual advantage regime over another—say, rampant capitalism over capitalism constrained by extensive social welfare programs—both of which are likely to be an improvement for virtually everyone over pure equality. Political philosophers might easily enough claim that we need political equality in some sense, but they will not be able to reckon what that means if the constituents of individuals' political power are anything like the disparate clutter of Rawls's primary goods.

Hence, we are returned to the original problem: how to balance equality with mutually advantageous inequality. The difference principle should have stopped the indeterminacy of mutual advantage, but it brings its own indeterminacy—not merely incompleteness, but incoherence. So far, we have only an idea that such balancing might rescue the urge for egalitarianism from the dismissals of Hume, Hayek, and others. We do not have a way to put such an idea into meaningful terms.

CONCLUDING REMARKS

Unless it is applied ex ante, the principle of mutual advantage is woefully conservative in many contexts. It allows only those changes that hurt no one or that fully compensate all those who are harmed by the change. Ex ante, all might be expected to benefit from, say, technological change—although we can be sure that ex post some will have lost, as peasants, farmers, Luddites, and modern high-tech firms such as IBM have sometimes lost. Hume supposes that we all benefit—"every individual person must find himself a gainer"—from having a legal regime of private property ([1739–40] 1978, bk. 3, pt. 2, sec. 2, 497). Mutual advantage applied as from today could hold the world hostage to a backward dictator or social class. But ex ante the principle is so broadly pleasing that the greatest of distributive justice theorists has accepted it in his theory of distributive justice. Since utilitarians also find it compelling, it may currently be the most widely accepted principle in Western moral and political philosophy. It is not sufficient to resolve all issues—it is too radically indeterminate for that—but neither fairness theorists nor utilitarians would significantly violate it.

There is a potential intellectual problem in the focus on mutual advantage. Historically, that has been the focus of philosophers now considered conservative. And, indeed, if the principle of mutual advantage is not viewed ex ante but in medias res, it is inherently conservative because it commends only those policies that do not make the wealthy (or anyone else) worse off. Mutual advantage in medias res would presumably be an acceptable theory for Marie Antoinette or Idi Amin. It is also seemingly the political theory of many contemporary libertarians and it, in the form of an initial unanimity rule, has been enunciated as the necessary starting point for any theorizing about policy (Buchanan and Tullock 1962). But even mutual advantage ex ante is associated primarily with conservatives such as Hobbes, for whom justice is merely a positive, and not a normative, term—it is what government achieves and, on his account, that will serve mutual advantage.

Henry Sidgwick (1907, 440) accused Hume of having a restricted vision, because Hume neglected distributive justice and discussed only justice as order (see further Hardin 1988, 36–37). In fact, before the radical utilitarians of the early-nineteenth century, distributive justice was only sometimes of concern. The very term meant, perversely to the modern ear, distribution of rewards and offices according to merit, as in Aristotle's concern with giving the persons with the best relevant characters the offices of leadership. Occasional appeals for egalitarianism, as in the writings of Gerrard Winstanley ([1652] 1973) during the English revolutionary period, were often grounded in an appeal to a particular kind of life, especially agrarian subsistence farming. This was a kind of life that was eventually doomed and that could have brought equality only by violating the possibilities of mutual advantage and the difference principle. Unfortunately for the long debate over mutual advantage and other theories of justice, the nonconservative tradition has often been hobbled by bad social science or has been anti-social-scientifically romantic.

Rawls has done political theory the great service of bringing the egalitarian and mutual-advantage principles together into one theory, where their effects can be debated constructively without dismissively consigning them to ideological out boxes turned it opposite directions. He has also helped bring institutions back into moral theory—although, in truth, he and his commentators are retrograde in focusing far more on psychology (or "moral psychology") than on recognizable institutions.[17] Utilitarian economists kept up the interest in institutional arrangements while philosophers neglected it through much of the twentieth century. But utilitarian economists were—often wrongly—lumped into the ideological world of, supposedly, Hobbes, where they could be ignored by those with egalitarian leanings. Again today, perhaps we can count on social scientists to keep us on track in the effort to understand justice and its workability by treating workability as an important concern independent of ideology.

Has Rawls succeeded in giving us a theory that improves on utilitarianism, as he wanted to do? He makes his comparison too easy by rejecting Hume's utilitarianism and focusing on the least-credible additive, "classical," Benthamite version of utilitarianism (20 [22]). Contemporary utilitarian political theory cannot be grounded in a trivially Benthamite value theory. Quite apart from metaphysical objections to making interpersonal comparisons, such as Pareto had, there are obvious epistemological difficulties that may be insurmountable. Utilitarians may still accept at least some interpersonal comparisons and some aggregations across persons, as the professedly antiutilitarian Rawls (xvii–xviii and passim [vii–viii and passim]; 1996, 178–87) says he does in his account of primary goods.[18] But for many matters in political philosophy, utilitarians must settle for either Hobbesian or Coasean efficiency—both of which are mutual-advantage, not greatest-good, conceptions—rather than aggregate welfare comparisons, and they must grant that the theory is indeterminate in many contexts. If utilitarians are not happy with Hobbes or Coase, they must attempt to define an alternative notion of dynamic efficiency that can lie at the core of their political theory. And if they do not improve on these, they face the perplexing problem that the Hobbesian foundationalist vision does not coherently connect with the Coasean marginalist vision.

Apart from the indeterminacy of mutual advantage that contemporary ordinal utilitarianism shares with Rawls's theory, however, such utilitarianism seems much less indeterminate than justice as fairness, with its incoherent collection of primary goods and its difference principle to bridge the misfit pair of mutual advantage and equality. Of course, as I will argue in chapter 8, the burdens of indeterminacy of both theories may be substantially reduced if they can call on institutions to handle many problems to achieve what might be called mechanical determinacy.

Chapter Eight

Mechanical Determinacy

OW DO WE LIVE with indeterminacy? In part through the devices canvassed in preceding chapters. For a very important range of issues in whole societal contexts, however, we set up institutions to deal with it. Indeed, at the end of a sound social theory stands an institution.[1] In personal contexts we simply live with indeterminacy, and *the passage of time renders personal choices determinate after theory fails.* The world is stochastic and so are our lives, and it and our lives are created out of our strategic interactions, with all their incumbent indeterminacies. In both personal and social contexts, we therefore often do not achieve theoretical determinacy, but only *mechanical determinacy.* Institutions may resolve our problems mechanically and they may even impose theory on us, as argued below for the institutional imposition of mutual advantage over alternative theories of criminal justice. And indeed, plumping for public policy in some contexts is tantamount to accepting—even insisting on—interpersonal comparisons.

Mutual advantage is a relatively compelling holistic normative principle for social organization—when it applies. This was Hobbes's use of it, although the principle will not yield Hobbes's determinate recommendations if we know even a bit of social science. Because we can differentially evaluate various forms of government—such as liberal democracy and fascist or communist autocracy—we cannot invoke a principle of insufficient reason to let us be equally content with the choice of any of these, as Hobbes asserted he was. In an ordinal welfarist theory, to say that all individuals are better off allows us to say that the society is better off. There is no fallacy of composition in such a claim so long as we suppose the latter statement is merely shorthand for the former. Unfortunately, all that the standard of mutual advantage yields us is such comparative claims as that state A is better than state B, while it may be indeterminate in the comparison of state A to state C and most other states.

Mutual advantage is arguably a less compelling normative principle for marginal changes. At the margin, exclusive resort to the principle is inherently conservative. Utilitarians can readily reject it if they think even rough interpersonal comparisons of welfare are possible (Hardin 1988, 53–59, 126–137). Mutual advantage is conservative in a sense different from that of George Stigler ([1959] 1965), who labels commitment to the market as conservative (that view makes the current radicals in east Europe and the former Soviet republics conservative). It is conservative in the traditional sense of obeisance to the status quo. Vast systemic changes, such as those currently underway in many of the eastern nations, cannot plausibly be considered mutually advantageous, because they will surely make many identifiable people or groups net losers.[2]

Can we resolve any of the indeterminacies that remain in efficiency theories? We might be able to do so if we can move part of the way toward Bentham or Posner's interpersonally comparable measures. The interpersonal comparisons we actually make are sometimes marginal, sometimes holistic. Marginally, we might say that my itch is less harmful than your broken leg or that my large raise in salary is less good than your finally getting a job. Holistically, we might say that your plentiful existence with long life prospects in a peaceful and productive society is better than my impoverished existence with short life prospects in a destitute and violent society. These are, in both the marginal and the holistic cases, merely ordinal comparisons.

We may think it better to make one life a bit less good in order to enhance the other substantially. Or, more systematically, we might think it good to transfer resources from a very well off class to a much poorer class. Here, however, we may not be able to do what Coase's theorem suggests we can (chapter 5). Coase first separates production from allocation to maximize production as measured in current prices, and then goes on to allocate benefits from the increased production. If changes in production are principally a matter of changing property inputs, Coase's move should work, subject as always to transaction costs. But if changes in production are very much a matter of changing labor inputs, especially in the form of greater commitment and human capital, then allocations may affect outputs. This is the problem that drives Rawls's difference principle, according to which we would consent to inequalities in rewards for work to the extent that those inequalities lead to greater production that benefits even the worst off in the society.

Finally, note that Posner is quite catholic in what he includes under wealth (chapter 4). Pareto's principles seem able to accommodate any values, although they cannot handle production. Coase is also catholic. True, his examples typically involve dollar amounts of costs and benefits to relevant parties, but the dollars are a device, not a value, and they can be traded for other things that have value. Moreover, he says we must be fairly broad in our accounting of welfare effects. He even cites, perhaps partly tongue in cheek, Frank Knight's view that problems of welfare economics must ultimately dissolve into a study of aesthetics and morals (Coase [1960] 1988, 154).

Unlike the modern writers, Hobbes seemed to prefer to keep economic and survival issues separate from nonmaterial issues. Why the difference? Perhaps it is just the development of utility theory, the most articulate and extensive of all value theories, over the past three centuries. Or perhaps because in the conditions of his time, Hobbes thought other concerns were swamped by the problem of survival and material prosperity. These were for him roughly what primary goods are for Rawls's theory. Before Hobbes's material goods are secured, he supposed people are not likely to invest heavily in many alternative values (Hobbes [1651] 1968, chap. 13, p. 186 [62]). To some extent, this is even a constitutive claim. For example, one cannot have a value for group identity in a Hobbesian state of nature. Hence, Hobbes's initial values of survival and welfare are prior to such socially determined values as identity and such political values as participation. It is because later theorists are writing about going societies that they can sensibly bring such values into their accounts, although it would be a mistake to give them priority, as is sometimes done. However, such other values cannot so plausibly be kept out of arguments about reform and revolution, unless one thinks the expected benefit of securing the right regime could never offset the expected risk of chaotic anarchy on the way to getting that regime.

We can conclude that various efforts to take us to the frontier of mutual benefit have greatly improved our understanding of the problems of ordinal welfarism, but they have not resolved all problems. Hobbes and Coase have proposed extraordinary moves that make the program of mutual advantage seem plausibly workable in some contexts, both holistic and marginal, but they still leave us with indeterminacies. To resolve these, we might impose at least ordinal interpersonal comparisons, which, however, violate the principle of mutual advantage from which Hobbes, Pareto, Coase, and much of law and economics have worked. Interpersonal comparisons might, however, provide a refuge for policy makers and judges faced with difficult issues or cases in which long-run efficiency is not likely to be affected by the present policy or decision.

MARGINALISM

There is a widely used vernacular sense in which conservatism merely favors the status quo, somehow defined, over change. In this sense, perhaps the conservatism both of economics and of law and economics is as much a theoretical as an empirical result. For more than a century, the dominant tradition in Western economics has been marginalist (Stigler 1982). In this tradition, there is no point in talking about the overall value of organizing society one way rather than another. Contemporary economics only provides vocabulary and theory for discussing the marginal value of a change. We are in the world of Hume, Pareto, and Coase, not in that of Hobbes or Bentham. This may be the right place to be, and we may conclude that economic conservatism is not merely empirically well grounded, but that it is theoretically incumbent on us.

Such an analysis does not, however, tell the whole story. In addition to empirical lessons and the appeal of theory, contemporary economics is built on a genuine value commitment. The value is marginalist welfarism with an uneasy mix of interpersonally noncomparable and interpersonally comparable elements. If welfarism were inherently marginalist, then *it* would be conservative. But the issue for an ordinal welfarism is not that the judgments are marginal in the sense of trivial or minor. Hobbes's holistic theory of the mutual advantage of having a state is welfarist, but it is not marginalist. That theory is conceptually coherent and even empirically plausible. Welfarism is therefore not inherently marginalist. Rather, it is only comparative or relative.

The genuinely conservative element of this line of theory is that it constrains change to what would be mutually advantageous—thereby ruling out supposed improvements that depend on trade-offs and aggregation of interpersonally comparable welfares. If we can only do what will be mutually advantageous, we automatically privilege the status quo. It is sometimes noted that utilitarianism was once the moral theory of political radicals and reformers, but that it is now the theory of conservatives (e.g., Williams 1972, 102–3). Indeed, it is the implicit moral theory of most Western economists and perhaps now of most Eastern economists as well. Part of the change is the abandonment of cardinal, interpersonally comparative utility theory, which for Eastern economists was a labor theory of value, on which a jerry-built economic theory was founded.

If the issue is the skepticism that leads to marginalism, Hobbes does not fit because he was unwilling to take up debate about marginal changes. In some ways, the most far-reaching skeptic in modern economics was Friedrich Hayek (1948b), who justified the decentralized market on the ground that the epistemology of a central organization could not match that of economic actors taken spontaneously together. Hayek (1960b, 408) claimed he was not a conservative, but was a Whig. In this claim he merely invoked the earlier vocabulary of economic liberalism to mean what Stigler meant by economic conservativism. Hayek, however, was intellectually inconsistent if his value theory was welfarist and not interpersonally comparative, because he clearly supposed that switching from nonmarket to market devices is good, although such a switch is likely to entail losses in welfare for some.

A commitment to mutual advantage might block intervention to help those who are—speaking with interpersonal comparisons of welfare—woefully worse off than the norm. It may be true, either for Stigler's empirical reasons or for theoretical reasons, that we cannot intervene in such cases without severe distortion of the larger economy, reducing its productivity and reducing the welfare of others. A modestly more generous value commitment that somewhat violates the collective implication of self-interest might allow such intervention anyway.

In an actual economy, we cannot even honor the Pareto principle. If there were enormously many sellers and buyers, my welfare would be unaffected by whether you are also a seller. But if I own the only restaurant at my intersection, and you open another across from me, I may be massively affected by your selling in my market. True, all of your transactions may be voluntary exchanges that benefit both you and your partners in transaction. But the result may not be to push all of us toward the frontier of mutually advantageous better allocation because it may reduce my welfare, it may even bankrupt me, merely because you are the better cook or have louder music.

Two-Stage Theory

In general, we face two quite separate problems of choice about collective matters. First, we create institutions and organizations to handle certain issues. Ex ante the creation of a particular institution may be genuinely mutually advantageous in our expectations (although the choice between alternative institutions may not be). Second, we—or our institutions—adopt specific policies and implement them. The choice and implementation of many actual policies will not be mutually advantageous. Our two choices, of institutions and of policies, are epistemologically analogous to a limited extent. Even though an institution might be expected by each person to be beneficial to herself, it may nevertheless be true that it would also be expected by everyone to bring net losses to some. My expectations of net benefit in such a case would be statistical. I might expect a range of possible effects on me, from net losses to net benefits, but with the expected value overall of net benefits.

Adopting an actual policy will be similar in the sense that it will be based on statistical expectations of the costs and benefits of the policy. Those expectations might, again, come from a range of possible outcomes for particular individuals, with some of them losing overall while others benefit. The difference between the two—creating a policy institution and adopting a policy— must often be that actual individuals might be surer of where they are likely to come out from the policy than from the institution. For example, a new policy of progressive taxation would affect many people in ways they could confidently predict. The two-stage move of creating institutions which then make microchoices and policies is a pragmatic variant of Rawls's veil of ignorance or of the principle of insufficient reason. An important aspect of it is that it blocks direct assessments of the rightness, wrongness, justice, or injustice of various states of affairs and actions.

Hume may have been the most insistent of all two-stage theorists after Hobbes. He blocks the direct application of utility to issues of ownership as a shortsighted violation of principles of justice:

> Cyrus, young and unexperienced, considered only the individual case before him, and reflected on a limited fitness and convenience, when he assigned the long coat to the tall boy, and the short coat to the other of smaller size. His governor instructed

him better, while he pointed out more enlarged views and consequences, and informed his pupil of the general, inflexible rules, necessary to support general peace and order in society. (Hume [1751] 1975, 304–5)

This passage is sometimes cited as proof that Hume was not a utilitarian or that he was a rule utilitarian. On the contrary, this argument is a necessary conclusion from an institutionally grounded utilitarianism. For solid utilitarian reasons, a law of property must be established in a working institution and must be applied to cases. That law should be designed to govern property relations in ways that enhance welfare. The content of that law must then be applied by various officials in any particular case without taking utilitarian assessments into account.

Also on this ground, Hume demolished Aristotle's and others' views of distributive justice based on merit as utterly impracticable. Focusing on the direct outcome of such distributive justice is not possible. Hence he supposed, "the civil magistrate very justly puts these sublime theorists on the same footing with common robbers, and teaches them by the severest discipline, that a rule, which, in speculation, may seem the most advantageous to society, may yet be found, in practice, totally pernicious and destructive" (Hume [1751] 1975, 193). In essence, he plumped for laissez-faire distributive justice. This is not quite the libertarian justice of, say, Robert Nozick (1974), because it depends merely on what happens and not on whether the way things happen meets some pristine libertarian or other principle. What the way things happen must do is fit an institutional structure for causing them generally to be utilitarian, meritocratic, or egalitarian.

If we are to follow a principle of, say, distribution by merit, we have to recognize, with Hume and Rawls (1955), that we must first create an institution designed to effect such a distribution. Every sensible theory of government must be a two-stage theory. Once a particular distribution has been reached by the best institution we can design (including all arrangements for appealing its decisions at various levels), the most that an Aristotelian or other meritocrat can do is say that things have worked out badly, not that we ought to try to do anything to change the distribution. Hume's fundamentally pragmatic criticisms of egalitarianism, reward by merit, and direct invocation of utility are compelling.

Despite these examples, the two-stage argument is not specifically about moral and justice issues. It is about all issues for which management requires organization. It is as true of people working in a factory as of roleholders in the government or the justice system that they should have their tasks defined by their fit with the organization's design to achieve its purpose. If I am working on an assembly line, I should do the task that has been designed for the larger purpose of the line. I should not idiosyncratically act on behalf of that larger purpose directly. I might grasp something about the way things are done that should be changed and might commend that change to those running the assembly line, but I generally should not unilaterally take action on my own (see further Hardin 1998a).

Similarly, an officer in the large and complex system of deterrence had a relatively particular role of participating in firing weapons and essentially no role in determining what the policy on deterrence should be or when the weapons were to be fired. Once the policy of deterrence was adopted, carrying it out well required the selection and training of people to fit specific roles for the execution of the policy. The "content" of those roles was not determined directly by the problem of deterrence but indirectly from the nature of the institution for carrying out the deterrence policy. Some role holders might have chosen to act according to values that contradicted the deterrence policy, but a well-designed system would have worked despite such occasional misfits with the design.

What makes the two-stage account compelling is that, first, complexity blocks individual mastery of various problems and, second, that individual interactions that are unconstrained would be vastly less fruitfully coordinated than interactions that are managed by an organization, which can stipulate how to coordinate. Imposing an organization on many complex activities is necessary if they are to be mastered at all by reducing the range of indeterminacies that would afflict unorganized activities.

It is very often likely to be true that we would be better served by imposing any one of many forms of organization on our joint activities than by leaving them to spontaneous regulation. When we do impose an organization on an activity or purpose, in part we do as Hobbes did. We simplify the complexity of our world enough to be able to master it. We do not genuinely eliminate all of the relevant indeterminacies when we select, fall into, or adapt one organizational form rather than various others, but we do allow ourselves to improve on our status quo ante by simply, mechanically overriding some of the indeterminacies of strategic interaction.

INSTITUTIONAL FALLIBILITY

One of the most important considerations in actual institutions is their fallibility. They may be misdesigned or, more ordinarily, they may be staffed with less than perfectly functioning agents.[3] They therefore often bring about results that fit poorly with their mandates. One might say it is part of the epistemology of an institution that it is fallible, sometimes in ways individuals are fallible, sometimes in ways in which institutions are distinctively and incorrigibly fallible. A well-designed institution is one that reduces the incidence of failure— but it typically can only reduce, not eliminate, this incidence. If institutions are fallible—inherently, predictably fallible—then that fact should enter into our principles for designing them. We may not be able to design out fallibility, but we might be able to design around it, in a sense, by building in checks and redundancies.

An institution can be inescapably fallible for the reason that we cannot design a better one. Charles Beitz supposes that an institutionally designed egalitarian voting scheme might actually leave someone in a less than equal voting position. Arguing from the structure of Rawls's more general theory of justice, Beitz (1989) concludes that this person would then have no further recourse to get the seeming injustice of the voting scheme corrected if the scheme is the best that can be done under the just theory of democratic participation. Similarly, Rawls's theory of just distribution offers no further corrective to the worst-off class once the institutions of justice have been properly designed. In these two cases, it seems that there is nothing further for the individuals to do or to claim against the larger society or its institutions. Why? Because the institutions are ideally designed, and they achieve the best that can be achieved, so that there is no further principle for corrective action. What might seem to be merely corrective action might severely undermine the institution that does the best possible.

More commonly, institutions fail even to meet the standards intended for them. What should individuals do when they think that the state is fallible and that it has brought about or allowed the wrong result? They should do just what they should do in general when they think the law is wrong. They should sometimes violate the law even knowing that the authorities may sanction them for their violation. It can be right for me to break a law that it would be right for the state to enforce just because individuals and institutions may have different epistemological capacities (Hardin 1994). Similarly, in some underlying sense of justice, it could be just for me to violate the distribution that an institutional principle of justice fallibly mandates.

For Hume, criminal and civil law were both mutually advantageous. Again, Sidgwick (1907, 440) called Hume's view of justice "justice as order." It is a mutual-advantage theory ex ante and should therefore fit easily enough with fundamental mutual-advantage arguments. Some defenses of criminal law are essentially defenses from justice as order. Others, such as theories of corrective justice or retributive justice, are not typically either theories of distributive justice or of justice as order. These theories therefore have the logical (and likely) possibility of conflicting with theories of distributive justice and with mutual-advantage theories. And theories of distributive justice have the possibility of conflicting with theories of mutual advantage, although Rawls's theory is intended to accommodate limited arguments for mutual advantage without incoherence.

I wish to argue something even more forceful and telling than this merely logical problem. Theories of distributive justice, retributive justice, and corrective justice (the last may be incoherent in any case) must generally *give way to* mutual advantage *in a real-world justification* of criminal law. In abstract theory one might argue against this conclusion. But in practice the conclusion seems unavoidable for stochastic reasons. This is not the relation between equality and mutual advantage as argued in chapter 7 for Rawlsian distributive justice, in which the mutual-advantage principle only modifies egalitarian determinations. Here, mutual advantage overrides principles of criminal justice.

Why is practice so harsh for theory? Recall the discussion of criminal justice in chapter 3 and the once commonplace claim that we should do justice though the heavens fall—*fiat justitia, ruat caelum*. This claim is silly even if it is read as merely pompously metaphorical. On the metaphorical reading, the claim says that if grievous harm will follow from doing justice, we should always nevertheless do justice and let the harm follow. This is often seen as an issue in the pluralism of values. But reality is harsher than this.

Suppose our theory of justice is anything other than merely mutual advantage. It follows that mutual-advantage considerations must potentially conflict with justice. Now consider a criminal justice system that is grounded in our more general theory of justice. Although we might not be certain of any particular case—except, perhaps, in the current wave of retrospective DNA tests—we are very nearly certain in principle that our courts occasionally *do* grievous injustices. I might nevertheless think it best that we have our fallible criminal justice system, even at the risk that it wrongly punish me, because, ex ante, I expect to be generally better off with such a system than without one. If everyone shares my view or my interests, then the system is mutually advantageous even though it might occasionally be unjust. Moreover, we might think it is not merely mutually advantageous—it is hugely advantageous, so much so that we think it is justified to trade its advantages for its injustices. Nobody but a rationalizing Pollyanna or former governor George Bush could suppose any actual working system of criminal justice does not occasionally produce unjust results (see Lovinger 1999; Firestone 1999). *Anyone who nevertheless supports an actual system of criminal justice therefore supports letting mutual-advantage considerations trump justice considerations to some extent.* Backed to the wall by the real world, virtually every moral and political theorist is an ex ante mutual-advantage pragmatist about criminal law.

Mutual-advantage theories are almost inherently institutionalist. (This claim is qualified by "almost" because David Gauthier [1986] has presented a mutual-advantage theory that is ostensibly not institutionalist but personal.) For example, it may not always be to our mutual advantage to refrain from murder. But it likely would be to our mutual advantage to have a relatively effective legal regime against murder. What makes it advantageous to me to be coerced not to murder or steal is that the coercion will not be specific to me but will be general, so that virtually all others also find it advantageous to themselves—under the regime of state coercion—not to murder or steal. Hence, there is mutual advantage in having a relevant legal regime.

The core concern of mutual-advantage theories is to allow for making our world better for us, not only fairer. Strangely, it may be easier to argue for the mutual advantage of a legal regime than to argue from any other perspective for its justice. To argue for the justice of a practical regime per se against murder, for example, requires that we construct it to achieve only—or almost only—correct convictions. At some point, of course, failure to convict any innocent person is tantamount to not convicting any guilty person either, hence tantamount to having no regime at all. We must, on our principles of justice, decide on a trade-off between convictions of the innocent and convictions of the guilty. If we do this, then at some point we are, again, arguing from mutual advantage rather than from justice.

Most theories of justice are not argued in ways that make this inference perspicuous. But a theory of mutual advantage could, in principle, easily handle the trade-off. I am better off at the point at which my losses from no regime outweigh the union of my gains from a regime (in the conviction of those who are guilty and deterrence of those who might become guilty) and my losses from it (in the mistaken conviction of me or others whom I would rather have protected). In actual application, the theory may not be so easy to work out, because our social-scientific account of the effects of various regimes may not be very good.

A central problem for a systematic theory of justice is how to fit it with other concerns, especially concerns that sometimes compete with (distributive) justice. We could say that justice always trumps, as in the hallowed but silly claim that we should do (legal or criminal) justice though the heavens should fall. The heavy burden for a pure theory of distributive justice is to *accommodate principles of criminal justice through fallible institutions* that will predictably take action against the innocent on occasion. And throughout we must be concerned to make it work with plausible real-world institutions. If such a theory cannot do this, it must inherently rule out practical criminal justice. If we insist on the perfect fairness of never convicting the innocent, we may have such faulty results that we all suffer. And if we insist on the equality of results that pure distributive justice might seem to require, we may also achieve far more dismal results than if we constrain our application of the equality principle in our collective interest.

One way for a theory of distributive justice to be made to fit with a theory of criminal justice would be to allow criminal verdicts to fit into the range of what is to be distributed. A member of the worst-off class would receive a lighter sentence for a particular crime than would a member of a better-off class. This move might be pleasing to hard-nosed egalitarians. It would reverse the more likely practice in our own law and the quite open norms of medieval European law, in which penalties for crimes were correlated inversely with status: the higher the status, the lower the penalty.

Where would mutual advantage stand on a status-based criminal law? If we are to choose between a medieval system, in which penalties varied enormously depending on social status, and a universalistically fair system, the principle of mutual advantage cannot be determinate unless sociology and psychology can show that we would all benefit from one over the other—a prospect that might seem implausible. Despite its superficial implausibility, however, it could be sociologically true that those in upper status positions would benefit enough from the society of egalitarian law for it to be in their interest to choose egalitarian law over caste law. Why? Because those of lower status might be far more productive and cooperative under a regime of fair law, enough so as to benefit those of higher status even after the latter give up their legal privileges. This result might be dependent on whether the law was relatively effective at suppressing illegal activities and on whether there were status differences in the effectiveness of law.

Perhaps the largest practical problem in a system of justice, however, is the combination of ordinary institutional and organizational problems with limits to individual rationality and commitment. These presumably often lie behind the problem that extant systems of justice sometimes go awry and punish the innocent. Among these problems, one that seems to have got too little attention looms very large. Although a system of criminal justice might readily be characterized as fitting with some more general theory of justice or with some specific principle of justice—mutual advantage, Rawlsian distributive justice, procedural justice, or retributive justice—its officers might follow very different principles, including their personal interest. Part of the problem of designing a good system of justice therefore is to design one that will work with the human material at hand. And part of the problem of arguing a good theory is to construct it to work well in the hands of actual humans.

Such workability was a central issue for James Madison and others in the drafting of the U.S. Constitution—to structure government so that it would work reasonably well even with knaves in office.[4] One of the most difficult problems in the criminal law under that constitution has been making law equitable even when the racism of its officers intrudes on their actions. A value as pervasive as American racism may be nearly impossible to constrain even in the law.

INSTITUTIONS AS MELIORATIVE

If the argument here is correct, institutions, unlike individuals, are generally forced to make meliorative moves that are not mutually advantageous. You and I can agree to act in ways that serve our mutual advantage without making any claims of interpersonal trade-offs. That is, indeed, the nature of ordinary exchange. I trade my X for your Y and we are both better off. Perhaps one could reasonably say that you are made much better off, while I am made only slightly better off. And perhaps one could even argue that we should not have exchanged but that you should merely have given me Y and that your gift would have made us jointly better off than our trade would have. Still, the trade is mutually advantageous and therefore utilitarian with respect to the status quo before the trade without any judgment of how much better off it makes the two of us together. Variance among the individuals that institutions address virtually guarantees that the institutional actions will not have this character in actual fact, because the institutions impose burdens on some and award benefits to others, even though an institution might be incapable of judging that its actions do impose net costs on any particular persons.

The role of courts of equity at their height in England was to handle the variant cases that were decided properly according to the law but that imposed supposedly unreasonable penalties on parties who were in some important respect unlike the standard parties before the law. One can imagine a similar device to accommodate claims that specialized knowledge outside the normal purview of an institution would justify special treatment of someone. But one cannot coherently expect that an institution be able to treat every case as special in this way and still do a good job of accomplishing its purpose of serving our interests. Hence, if an institution adopts a policy of allowing special appeals to "equity," it must likely do so only for extreme cases, not for relatively close calls. Their capacity for streamlining and standardizing decision making is a very important part of what makes institutions useful to us. We cannot simultaneously wreck their standard procedures and expect them to continue to be as useful. Again, ex ante it is plausibly mutually advantageous that we create such institutions even though, in specific instances of their acting, they may inflict net costs on some and we know ex ante that it is extremely likely that they will do so.

One might wish to say that melioration approximates to mutual advantage in such contexts. But this does not overcome the fact that it is not actually equivalent to mutual advantage and that it requires de facto trade-offs across individuals. Hence, a rigorous Paretian must oppose public policy altogether. The only genuinely rigorous Paretians in print are very hard-nosed libertarians, some of whom think we would manage to be as prosperous without institutions as we are with them. They therefore disagree fundamentally with Hobbes, whom they should see as their most threatening intellectual opponent. I think Hobbes has far the better case to make, even though he may exaggerate the extent to which efforts at reform threaten massive destruction from civil war and anarchy (Hobbes [1651] 1968, chap. 30, p. 380 [177]).

The general run of economists who claim to have inherited Pareto's value theory and who sometimes assert the impossibility of making interpersonal comparisons of welfare are not always Paretian in actual practice. They regularly prescribe both institutions and policies; they are the authors of cost-benefit analysis; and they may be next after lawyers in their representation in governmental councils. The ardor with which economists have defended the impossibility of interpersonal comparisons is more than matched by the energy with which they have urged policies requiring trade-offs that could be normatively grounded, if at all, only on the assumption of such comparisons.[5] Their inconsistency is no proof of the correctness or incorrectness of making such trade-offs. But if Hobbes is even roughly right, the impossibility of escaping the stasis of ex ante failure to adopt institutions for collective purposes is a powerful argument *for* the correctness of such trade-offs and of the de facto interpersonal comparisons they imply.

This conclusion suggests a slightly tricked-up justification of such comparisons. Ex ante, we all would want a better regulated world in which life would be much better for most of us and, in our ex ante expectations, even for each of us. Once we have the institutions for such regulation, we cannot practically escape making trade-offs between individuals—perhaps often unidentified and even unidentifiable individuals, but trade-offs nevertheless. *We cannot have the institutions that are ex ante justifiable unless we also take the eventual trade-offs. By ex ante mutual advantage argument, we ought to have those institutions. Hence, we ought also to have the trade-offs.* One of two contrary conclusions follows. The first is that the *rectitude*—moral and pragmatic, not metaphysical—of interpersonal trade-offs follows from an argument grounded only in mutual advantage. The second is that we should not have institutions at all because we cannot make interpersonal comparisons.

The second of these conclusions could be taken as an implication of the doctrine that "ought" implies "can." If we metaphysically cannot make interpersonal comparisons, then we ought not. Hence, we also ought not justify a system that depends on making such comparisons, and we should junk institutions. The first and contrary conclusion could be taken as an injunction to condone trade-offs or, even more strongly, to take interpersonal comparisons seriously. I concur with the stronger version of this conclusion. I think we should (and do) take interpersonal comparisons seriously. I do not have a metaphysical argument to establish how such comparisons can be given meaning in principle or an epistemological argument to show how we can know another's welfare to compare it to our own. I even agree with Pareto that we do not know what addition of utility or welfare across individuals means and nevertheless think we should do it.

The weaker version of the conclusion seems incontrovertible: We ought to condone interpersonal trade-offs. The alternative—to suppose we ought not have institutions to enhance welfare—is preposterous. Faced with the comparative difficulties of supposing we ought not have such institutions and of supposing we ought to condone the requisite interpersonal trade-offs, one who is motivated by the pragmatics of living well—for oneself and for others—must find the latter difficulty less implausible than the former. It is ex ante mutually advantageous to have institutions that make such trade-offs. Such institutions produce a mechanical determinacy in the face of pervasive indeterminacies.

Finally, note that a self-interest and a normative-mutual-advantage account of a social order might not be as far apart as one might at first suppose. Because mutual advantage is the ordinal, aggregate-level implication of individual-level self-interest, we can expect substantial effort and backing to produce an order that serves mutual advantage. In an actual society, what we may find is merely the achievement of the sociological variant of mutual advantage. All groups that are politically efficacious must be reasonably well served or they will tend to block the order or to work against it. Hence, the order will tend to serve the mutual advantage of all such groups (Hardin 1999d, chap. 1). Groups that are not politically efficacious may not be well served.

In a liberal, democratic society, one can perhaps expect a tendency for a sociologically mutual-advantage order to become more inclusive and to represent diverse groups. At least some of the institutions that protect and benefit the politically efficacious groups may come to protect and benefit others as well, especially if the way those institutions work is through direct application to individuals rather than to their groups as such. Liberal and democratic claims will not readily fit group membership. Still, some are likely to be left out of the larger benefits of the order.

CONTRACTARIAN ARGUMENTS

Social contract theory arose a few centuries ago from Hobbes, Locke, and others. For Locke and most others, the central concern was justification of government. For Hobbes, contract was merely a device to get to a government that provided order. Few contractarians or, as some now prefer to be called, contractualists are Hobbesian in this respect. Virtually all are Lockean. There is good reason for this, because contract has no role for Hobbes other than the causal one of creating government initially. And it is hardly necessary even for that role, which, indeed, Hobbes ([1651] 1968, chap. 20) thought was more likely to be played by usurpation or conquest. Hobbes ([1651] 1968, "Review and Conclusion," 722 [392]) noted that "there is scarce a Common-wealth in the world, whose beginnings can in conscience be justified."

Hobbes is often taken to have given us a justification of the state, but his text belies this entirely if this is meant to imply normative justification of any actual state from its origins. The causal role of the social contract has been nil. For Locke its role is philosophical and normative and, somehow, therefore deep even though it still cannot justify any actual states. Social contract theory has to do with voluntary agreement of some kind. For Locke agreement was right-making and the fact of our agreement in it justifies our government. For

Hobbes agreement was merely enabling, and the role of agreement was to select a sovereign so that the sovereign could bring order.

In various contexts here, I have often referred to what we would want or agree to, especially ex ante. In every case, what is at issue is what would serve our interests. Hence, the point is Hobbesian, not Lockean. For example, I generally take the fact of mutual advantage to be part of the explanation of where we are because it gives us incentives to go there. Although these incentives need not trump incentives to do otherwise, institutions and practices that finally are successful in serving mutual advantage do typically trump contrary incentives. Very often, as noted above, we will achieve only sociological, not complete mutual, advantage. Those with greater clout will be well served, while those with less may even be left out of many beneficial arrangements. This is mechanical determinacy with a vengeance, the determinacy of politics. Often we may do better than this and create institutions that, as seen ex ante, are not overwhelmingly biased in serving some groups far better than others.

Concluding Remarks

Often we defend our utopian claims as ideal theory. Such theory prescribes what we aspire to but what might be institutionally difficult or even virtually impossible to achieve for practical reasons. Such an argument cannot stand in the face of genuine indeterminacy on which some theory falters, however, because such indeterminacy renders the theory not merely difficult of achievement, but incoherent. Its failure is not pragmatic, but conceptual. There is no sense, for example, in which we can defend a democratic theory which requires that collective choice has the properties of individual choice. Arrow's theorem shows that this aspiration is incoherent. Similarly, any hope that we may find determinate theories of choice in the iterated prisoner's dilemma, in William Riker's size principle (see Hardin 1976), and, finally, in Rawls's theory of justice as fairness is forlorn, because all of these are indeterminate.

The better utopian ground for any argument that we must attempt to create determinate theories for fundamentally indeterminate contexts is that these wrong theories may help others to reframe the problems in ways that eventually are built on the genuine indeterminacy in manifold ways. The simplifications of Hobbes, Bentham, Pareto, Rawls, and others are valuable missteps. Pareto ([1927] 1971, chap. 3, sec. 31, p. 111) said of earlier, mistaken theories in economics that "it would be a serious error to think that it would have been a good thing had these erroneous theories never seen the light of day. These or other similar ones were indispensable in order to arrive at better theories." And of the mistaken theorists, he said, "We cannot blame them, because, briefly, questions must be resolved one after the other, and it is always better not to hurry" (chap. 4, sec. 11, pp. 183–84).

In our slow pace toward better theory in many contexts, both individual level and societal level, we should often attempt to recognize relevant indeterminacies at the outset, even in the fundamental assumptions of our theories. Doing so leads to more compelling theories in the case of the iterated prisoner's dilemma, in the foundations of social order, in the Rawlsian vision of distributive justice, and in manifold contexts in between these, in particular in the two-stage theory of organizing the resolution of complex problems of many and varied kinds. It also seems to commend the use of rough interpersonal comparisons in many contexts.

For theory that is grounded in micro interactions, the most difficult problem we face is the pervasive indeterminacy of strategic interaction. The nature of strategic choice—choosing a strategy that admits many possible outcomes as opposed to choosing an outcome—violates simplistic visions of the nature of action and of prescriptions to act in certain ways rather than to attempt to achieve certain ends. The great debate over consequentialist versus deontological moral theories has been cast as a purely moral issue. It is first and foremost a conceptual issue, and the slightest conceptual analysis wrecks the deontological program. Policy issues inherently bring in strategic and stochastic problems that make nonsense of that program, and yet these are often fundamentally moral issues, as in the program to eradicate smallpox at the gruesome risk of enabling the worst epidemic in human history or the policy of nuclear deterrence with its similar range of possible results from the idyllic to the very grim.

The indeterminacy of strategic interaction is a problem that faces institutions both internally and externally as much as it does individuals externally. For example, a policy toward some group is likely to provoke external responses of changed behavior that then affect the value of the policy. More generally, policies are likely to have unintended consequences. This may sometimes be merely because policies, as is true of actions generally, commonly provoke responses. But it may also sometimes be because indeterminacies make it difficult or even impossible to say how strategic interactions will turn out.

There have been at least two very successful devices for dealing theoretically with indeterminacy in ways that yield determinate or very nearly determinate results: the holistic device of Hobbes and the marginal device of Coase. There have been many failing devices, which include asserting determinacy, arguing for equilibrium in complex interactive contexts, claiming cardinal, interpersonally comparative welfare, and recurring to a limited set of rules, as well as the partially failing, oddly complex simplifications of Rawls's theory of distributive justice. Facing up to indeterminacy is very productive in iterated prisoner's dilemma, game theory more generally, Arrow's theorem, Hobbes's resolution of social order, and the two-stage theory of organizations and their outputs.

A problem with rational choice accounts of behavior is that people often do not understand how different strategies affect their interests. This should not be surprising. Game theory was invented (or discovered?) less than a century ago, and probability theory is less than four hundred years old. Strategic and stochastic thinking are hard. Indeed, they are hard even for those who are sophisticated theorists of them. However, people are not especially good at understanding causal relations either, and yet they manage to get through life most of the time. Our task in explaining their successes and failures is often the task of understanding how they choose to deal with indeterminacies that often swamp reason.

Appendix to Chapter Two

Determinacy in Iterated Prisoner's Dilemma

From the symmetry of the players in an iterated prisoner's dilemma over a fixed number of plays, a determinate theory must prescribe the same strategy to each player. We may suppose it permits mixed strategies, so long as these are well defined. If it prescribes cooperation on the final, nth (n >> 1) play of the series, either player can do better by violating the theory and defecting in that play. Similarly, suppose that, on the final play, it prescribes a probabilistic mix of strategies, $pC + (1 - p)D$, where C is cooperation, D is defection, and $1 > p > 0$. Then either player can do better (in expected payoff) by defecting on that play. If it prescribes defection on all plays after some number q ($n > q > 1$) with cooperation or a mix of cooperation and defection on play $q - 1$, then either player can do better by defecting on play $q - 1$. Hence, the theory cannot prescribe either cooperation or a mix of cooperation and defection on the final play, and it cannot prescribe either of these on any play that precedes a final series of one or more defections. It must therefore prescribe defection on every play.

Individually Cardinal Utility

Cardinality of values was brought back into favor in the twentieth century for the individual's utility function in the analysis of risky choices.[1] Von Neumann and Morgenstern assumed a utility that has virtually the properties of money in their game theory. Under criticism for this seemingly retrograde vision in the great era of the ordinal revolution, von Neumann offered a proof that from an individual's ordinal rankings of various states, a cardinal set of values can be determined. His proof was simple.

Suppose I can rank any outcome, including lotteries over outcomes. Consider three outcomes. I rank A as better than B and B as better than C. Assign a value of 1 to A, the best of these outcomes, and 0 to C, the least attractive of the outcomes. I can also rank any probabilistic mix of A and B. For example, suppose I am offered the lottery $pA + (1 - p)C$. I can rank it between A and C. Because A has a value of 1 and C has a value of 0. Now I need only find the value of p for which I would be indifferent between getting the outcome B and getting the outcome $pA + (1 - p)C$. It has a value of pA, which is simply p. Hence, beginning with only ordinal valuations, I have produced a cardinal scale over my possible choices.

There is a severe epistemological problem with this theory. I am supposed simply to have in my brain the capacity to make fine judgments about the relative values to me of various outcomes. If you give me an outcome, I am able to say what weighted combination of any pair of outcomes—one of which I value more than I value yours and one of which I value less than yours—I would find of equal value to the outcome you offer. The demands of the theory far surpass what most of us seem likely able to do.

Even supposing this problem could be mastered, however, for our purposes here, the theory offers no help in resolving indeterminacies of collective choice. My cardinal range need bear no relation to yours even if we are comparing the same states of affairs. Von Neumann's trick therefore did not actually answer the early economic critics of game theory. It did not even make sense of the interpersonally comparable and interchangeable utility of the payoffs of games, and this is what early, cardinal game theory required. These payoffs are sometimes called money-metric utility. The very concept of, say, a zero-sum game makes sense only if my payoff and yours can be combined to yield a total of zero. This requires both a zero point for each of our scales and also interpersonal comparability. A realistic game theory must finally have ordinal rather than cardinal payoffs. But an ordinal game theory is far less tractable than a cardinal game theory. It shares the problem of indeterminacy that burdens collective choice generally.

How does von Neumann's cardinalization fit with the problems of the subjective utility theory discussed above? It has to be applied to whole states of affairs, not to piecemeal changes in the overall state of affairs. This is not helpful. Unfortunately, if we push the ordinal welfare theory very hard, we will find that it too makes sense only in application to whole states of affairs, not to bits of states of affairs. To say I prefer Mexican to Chinese food tonight is to say I prefer Mexican to Chinese food *all else held constant*. That, of course, means we are not ranking the changes at the margin but, rather, one arrangement of everything at once as compared to other arrangements of everything at once. In doing this, we take into account all complementarities and substitutabilities.

NOTES

CHAPTER 1: INDETERMINACY

1. There were two major vaccines available. One of these, by Jonas Salk, used a killed polio virus and the other, by Albert Sabin, used a live but attenuated virus. From the Sabin live vaccine it was possible but not very often likely that the vaccinated person would contract the virus; from the killed Salk vaccine it was not possible to contract the disease. The former was, however, thought to have advantages that out-weighed its slight risks. Principal among these was its conferral of herd immunity, which is immunity to others from contact with one who was recently vaccinated.

2. The morass and variety of solution theories in game theory, as represented already in von Neumann and Morgenstern, *Theory of Games and Economic Behavior* ([1944] 1953), is a perversely beautiful display of indeterminacy. Roughly two-thirds of that book is given over to analyses of particular types of games to which there might be a solution under some rule.

3. There is a related principle at the foundation of the libertarian vision of property rights. Locke supposed it right to assign rights of ownership over any natural object or parcel of land to the first person to make use of it. Locke argues that "every Man has a *Property* in his own *Person*." Hence, "The *Labour* of his Body, and the *Work* of his Hands, we may say, are properly his. Whatsoever he then removes out of the State that Nature hath provided, and left in it, he hath mixed his *Labour* with, and joyned to it something that is his own, and thereby makes it his *Property*. . . . For this *Labour* being the unquestionable Property of the Labourer, no Man but he can have a right to what that is once joyned to, at least where there is enough and as good left in common for others" (Locke [1690] 1988, par. 27). The final proviso, which is now commonly called Locke's proviso, may seem today to vitiate the theory, but when "all the World was *America*" (par. 49), the "*appropriation* of any parcel of *Land*, by improving it" was no "prejudice to any other Man, since there was still enough, and as good left; and more than the yet unprovided for could use. So that in effect, there was never the less left for others because of his inclosure for himself" (par. 33). In this state of affairs, prior to exchange, no one was in conflict for the basic good of unimproved land. The Pareto criteria would be rationally unobjectionable (but otiose) only in a world as primitive as that seen by Locke when all the world was America. In such a world, I could be made better off without any effect on your welfare, even *without any effect on your opportunities in the future*. This is, of course, an idyll, and not only because there were Indians on that American land. In very distant prehistory, perhaps all the world very nearly was America in Locke's sense, but then there might not have arisen any idea of property in land. The point of the idea of property is to deal with shortage.

4. There are other difficulties in the use of the Pareto criteria that will be addressed in chapter 3. Finally, note that the standard representation of the Pareto principles with

of ten victims in slightly under two years, while the rate of survival in the field on the ground is about one in ten—suggests that one might sooner have a heart attack in a properly equipped airplane than in any other place except a very good cardiac hospital (see Wade 1999). Hence, the fear of tort suits based on an assertion that defibrillators have been misused and have caused death has faded and the Federal Aviation Administration has recently ordered U.S. carriers to be equipped with defibrillators ("F.A.A. Orders Defibrillators on Airlines," *New York Times*, 15 April 2001, 1.19)

8. Some people might suppose that they themselves would be strengthened by their commitment to self-reliance and they might therefore prefer not to have a safety net for themselves. For Kant's argument, see Kant [1785] 1964, 423; see also Herman 1993, chap. 3 (essay first published in 1984).

CHAPTER 5: MARGINAL DETERMINACY

1. See the diagram and the accompanying discussion of Pareto in chapter 1.

2. If the cardinal value of my holdings is, say, $1,000 and I benefit from an ordinal improvement, then my new cardinal value must be $1,000 + x, where x is a positive cardinal value.

3. Some libertarians think life under anarchy much more benign and productive than Hobbes thought it could be, and they suppose money would arise spontaneously even without government. Indeed, money has arisen in this way in the context of states and well-ordered societies. But when it does come into being, money has the characteristic that it is relevant to marginal values, not to the grand comparisons that interest Hobbes.

4. As followers of recent debates about the research and conclusions of Napoleon Chagnon (1968) on the Yanomami know, the view of their warlike behavior is contested. See, among many other recent commentaries, Tierney 2000; Ferguson 1995; Geertz 2001; Mann 2001; Wong 2001. The most recent views may be found at Yanomami.com.

5. See further, Hardin 1992a, where the argument is strictly welfarist rather than Benthamite utilitarian. But the argument turns on the overwhelming knowledge and theory demands for making more than marginal claims.

6. Fuller (1969, 132–33) even argues that laws that are not facilitative but that attempt to block voluntary mutual choices, such as laws against crimes without victims, fail because their morality as law is wrong. Contrariwise, law can be very well used to enforce morality in promise-keeping.

CHAPTER 6: RULES FOR DETERMINACY

1. Kant's strictures against masturbation and suicide are not grounded in concern for social interaction.

2. Matson says further, "Surely no one will undertake to defend Kant's conclusion. Hence, if that conclusion really follows from his theory, then that theory is convicted of absurdity or worse." According to student notes of his university lectures, a younger Kant held less consistent, more humane views on lying under duress (see Kant 1963, 226–29).

3. For a mere hint of the vastness of the literature on promise keeping, see Hardin (1988, 42–43, 46–47, 48–49, 59–65).

4. This is the standard objection to the generalization argument and to the answer it is supposed to give to the question, What if everybody did that? If everybody lied with impunity, that would be bad. But if the generally honest Schindler lied to protect lives, that is not bad. For further discussion of the generalization argument, see Hardin 1988, 65–68.

5. One might suppose that such a generalization argument would work in Kant's kingdom of ends (or society of perfectly rational beings). But it is hard to imagine just what these beings would be like. Would they like and dislike each other, fall in love and fall out of love with one another? If so, then the Nagel test might still say we should not always tell the truth. If it did not include the possibilities for special friendships and romantic love, perhaps a society of perfectly rational people would not be very pleasing and any morality specifically fitted to it might be unfit for our world.

6. One might try to bring the problem of vaccination under Kant's principle of benevolence. That principle is not conceived to address stochastic problems such as those in which the ostensibly benevolent action may benefit some but harm others, but rather to address essentially determinate problems such as those in which one's benevolent action has a clear and de facto sure benefit for a particular person or persons.

7. You might know very well for yourself and for certain other parents who will and who will not have their children vaccinated. But the authorities are in no position to know much more than that certain communities or social groups are more likely than others to take the effort to protect their children. It is a claim of institutional ignorance that justifies invocation of the principle of insufficient reason because it is an institution that faces the decision whether to use Salk or Sabin vaccines for the public vaccination program.

8. See many contributions to the special issue on Ethics and Nuclear Deterrence, *Ethics* 95, no. 3 (April 1985).

9. I have discussed these two issues for utilitarianism in Hardin 1988, chapters 3 and 4.

CHAPTER 7: INDETERMINATE JUSTICE

1. In this chapter only, all page references to *A Theory of Justice* will be in (parentheses) for the revised 1999 edition and, where there are comparable passages, in [brackets] for the original 1971 edition. All other references in this chapter will be given with standard author-date information plus page reference where relevant.

2. A static theory of justice in this sense is that of Ackerman (1980), whose concern is solely to allocate manna from heaven, not to produce it.

3. In comparison to fairness and utilitarian theories, libertarianism, communitarianism, and various religious theories are side shows in contemporary Western political philosophy. Of these, libertarianism has been worked out most extensively, especially by Robert Nozick (1974), perhaps because it has liberal roots in Locke and the Scottish Enlightenment. Nozick's articulation of the theory, however, is almost entirely normative and is irrelevant to our messy real world.

4. In an astonishing statement, Rawls (13 [14]) says "that the principle of utility [meaning utilitarianism] is incompatible with the conception of social cooperation among equals for mutual advantage." Here he means classical Benthamite utilitarianism, in which utilities to all are added to reach a maximum sum. Mutual advantage is

the central utilitarian principle of Hume. Unfortunately, under "mutual advantage" in Rawls's index, one is referred to "reciprocity," which is not the meaning of mutual advantage in his theory, although it is a way to achieve mutual advantage.

5. Hume also argued that, "Perfect equality of possessions, destroying all subordination, weakens extremely the authority of the magistracy, and must reduce all power nearly to a level, as well as property." This sounds like an aristocratic concern, implying that hierarchy, and hence material inequality, is virtually necessary for achieving many desirable social goals, including governance. Many of the views of Hume cited here were first expressed in Hume's *Treatise of Human Nature* ([1739–40] 1978), but they are more accessibly and often more clearly stated in his *Enquiry Concerning the Principles of Morals* ([1751] 1975).

6. Because it cannot handle the substitutabilities and complementarities of various goods (Samuelson 1974).

7. This rule is not yet complete, because there might be more than one state in which the worst-off class is best off but with different distributions to others not in the worst-off class. One could state a stepwise rule that would be determinate up to any identically ranked alternative states (72 [83]).

8. Brian Barry (1989) generally seems to view equality as the main concern. This may be true as to the motivation for constructing the theory, but justice as fairness is logically dependent on both mutual advantage and equality working in tandem. Both are required, and Rawls's concern with how to bring them together leads to his distinctive difference principle.

9. Or, rather, among all of those states in which everyone is equally well off, Rawls's initial state is that state in which they are best off.

10. If the side payments are not less than—or at most equal to—the additional resources they lead to, there is no reason to make them.

11. Rawls implicitly acknowledges this point in his principle of fairness that has me compensate others when our choice of how to organize the society rewards my talents more and theirs less than some other form of organization would.

12. This virtually follows from the fact that the concern with material inequality long predates the modern concern with political equality. For example, William Paley ([1785] 1978, bk. 3, pt. 1, chap. 2, p. 95) argued for a welfarist difference principle more than two centuries ago.

13. For discussion of equality of political power, see Christiano 1996.

14. It is unfortunate that Rawls has stimulated use of the phrase "respect for persons." Such clever phrases in ethics seem almost always to be persuasive definitions. They sound good, but there is often little or no content to them. This phrase has become a shibboleth of our time. To speak or write the words is to reveal one's allegiance, not one's thought. Utilitarians insist that each person is to count as one and one only, a principle that sounds like equal respect for each person. Rawlsians say utilitarianism fails to take seriously the distinction between persons when it aggregates their welfare in a way that makes some worse off in order to make others better off (24, 153–60, 163 [27, 175–83, 187]). This verges on philosophical trash talk. (Greater Boston is the home of Larry Byrd, one of the greatest trash talkers.) Rawls's ordering of society does an analogous thing when it elevates one arrangement of society above another—even though my class is better off in the former and is made worse off in the latter—for the sake of meeting the conditions of the difference principle. If aggregative utilitarianism

violates respect for persons by submerging the individual's interests into the societal outcome, then Rawls's theory of justice similarly violates respect for persons. I think aggregative utilitarianism, which Rawls criticizes, is incoherent because interpersonally cardinally additive utility makes little sense at the micro level. But it does not in any distinctive sense lack respect for persons.

15. Rawls's views here are changed from the original statement, which ranks these goods—liberties and economic goods—in serial order (in the order of the list above) and forbids any "exchanges between basic liberties and economic and social gains" [63]. Compare the later edition (55), which deletes this constraint. The result is heightened inconsistency in the later edition, which (perhaps inadvertently) continues the earlier restriction in some passages (e.g., 182). This restriction is contrary to the way many sensible people in poor circumstances would choose. Rawls's own later misgivings are therefore apt. Mack the Knife, in Bertolt Brecht's "Threepenny Opera," put the point well: first comes food and then morality (or, we could add, self-respect). (Brecht 1955, 99, finale of the second act.) Material satisfactions rank fourth in Rawls's list of primary goods. Yet he seems to agree with Mack the Knife's higher ranking of welfare when welfare levels are dismal (55, 217).

16. The footnote refers to the problem of indexing among the primary goods (Rawls 1996, 180–81n). This problem is suggested in a much earlier reference to criticisms by Alan Gibbard (xix [x]).

17. A rare exception is the account of the institution of elections in Beitz 1989. That book was published more than a decade ago, and it is still a rare exception. Given the frequency of claims by Rawls and his commentators that his is a theory for setting up institutions, this is a disappointing fact.

18. On his response to utilitarianism, see also Rawls 1996, xvi–xvii, 162. Rawls seems to say that the general welfare cannot be part of an overlapping consensus because, roughly, it is too difficult to calculate (161–62). On the contrary, there is probably no concern that fits more nearly universally into an actual overlapping consensus than prosperity and even increasing prosperity. Indeed, for the world to which we might suppose Rawls's theory most readily applies—the North Atlantic community of the past century or so—prosperity must be among the very most consensually held values, more consensually even than the norm of one-person, one-vote. Not everyone everywhere seeks or wants prosperity, and certainly many political leaders—e.g., the Taliban and many other fundamentalist religious leaders—do not seem to want it for their citizens, and Gerrard Winstanley ([1652] 1973) and the Levellers did not want it for England in their day. But in many societies it is hard to imagine what would gain the support of more people than prosperity gains. An especially effective political slogan in the United States has been, "It's the economy, Stupid."

CHAPTER 8: MECHANICAL DETERMINACY

1. This may not be true of some social theories—and one must wonder about them, must even wonder whether they have any meaning.

2. We might nevertheless explain these changes sociologically on the claim that they do serve the mutual advantage of politically effective groups (see Hardin 1999d, chaps. 1 and 5).

3. This is, metaphorically, the central problem of Kantian ethics, as discussed in chapter 6. It is derived for a community of ideally rational agents, but it is to be applied in our world, which is clearly staffed with less than perfectly functioning (rational) agents.

4. Hume ([1742] 1985, 42) argues that in designing government, "every man must be supposed a knave."

5. Presumably, their fees for the latter vastly exceed anything they have earned for the former.

APPENDIX TO CHAPTER 4: INDIVIDUALLY CARDINAL UTILITY

1. The discussion of this issue adds nothing to the understanding of our general problem of the use of cardinal valuation of some kind to escape indeterminacy. The discussion can be skipped without loss. It is added here in order to dismiss this variant of cardinal utility from further consideration, despite the fact that this one variant of cardinal utility is meaningful enough in approximation for us actually to use it in certain contexts.

REFERENCES

Ackerman, Bruce A. 1980. *Social Justice in a Liberal State*. New Haven: Yale University Press.

Arrow, Kenneth J. [1951] 1963. *Social Choice and Individual Values*. 2nd ed. New Haven: Yale University Press.

———. 1973. "Some Ordinalist-Utilitarian Notes on Rawls's Theory of Justice." *Journal of Philosophy* 70 (May 10): 245–63.

———. 1978. "Nozick's Entitlement Theory of Justice." *Philosophia* 7 (June): 265–79.

———. 1983. *Collected Papers*. Vol. 1, *Social Choice and Justice*. Cambridge: Harvard University Press.

Aumann, Robert J. 1985. "What Is Game Theory Trying to Accomplish?" Pp. 28–76 in Kenneth J. Arrow and Seppo Honkapohja, eds. *Frontiers of Economics*. Oxford: Basil Blackwell.

Barry, Brian. 1980. "Is It Better to Be Powerful or Lucky?" *Political Studies* (June and September 1980) 28:183–94, 338–52.

———. 1989. *Theories of Justice*. Berkeley and Los Angeles: University of California Press.

———. 1995. *Justice as Impartiality*. Oxford: Oxford University Press.

Barry, Brian, and Russell Hardin, eds. 1982. *Rational Man and Irrational Society?* (Beverly Hills, CA: Sage Publications.

Beitz, Charles R. 1989. *Political Equality: An Essay in Democratic Theory*. Princeton: Princeton University Press.

Bentham, Jeremy. [1789] 1970. *An Introduction to the Principles of Morals and Legislation*. Edited by J. H. Burns and H.L.A. Hart. London: Methuen.

Berlin, Isaiah. 1976. *Vico and Herder: Two Studies in the History of Ideas*. London: Hogarth.

Bicchieri, Cristina. 1988. "Self-Refuting Theories of Strategic Interaction: A Paradox of Common Knowledge." *Erkenntnis* 11:1–17.

Bilder, Richard. 1985. "Formal Treaties and Tacit Agreements." *Bulletin of the Atomic Scientists* (April): 51–53.

Binmore, Ken. 1991. "Review of *Morality within the Limits of Reason*." *Economics and Philosophy* 7 (1): 112–19.

Bok, Sissela. 1978. *Lying: Moral Choice in Public and Private Life*. New York: Pantheon.

Brecht, Bertolt. 1955. *Die Dreigroschenoper*. In *Stücke* (Plays), vol. 3. Berlin: Suhrkamp Verlag.

Brennan, Geoffrey, and James M. Buchanan. 1985. *The Reason of Rules: Constitutional Political Economy*. Cambridge: Cambridge University Press.

Brzezinski, Zbigniew. 1983. *Power and Principle*. New York: Farrar, Straus, and Giroux.

Bruni, Frank. 1999. "Behind Police Brutality: Public Assent." *New York Times*, 21 February, sec. 4.

Buchanan, James M., and Gordon Tullock. 1962. *The Calculus of Consent*. Ann Arbor: University of Michigan Press.

Calabresi, Guido. 1985. *Ideals, Beliefs, Attitudes, and the Law*. Syracuse, NY: Syracuse University Press.

Campbell, Jeremy, 2001. *The Liar's Tale: A History of Falsehood*. New York: Norton.

Carritt, David. 1947. *Ethical and Political Thinking*. Oxford: Oxford University Press.

Chagnon, Napoleon. 1968. *Yanomamö: The Fierce People*. New York: Holt, Rinehart and Winston.

Christiano, Thomas. 1996. *The Rule of the Many: Fundamental Issues in Democratic Theory*. Boulder, CO: Westview Press.

Clines, Francis X. 2001. "Furor Anew with Release of Man Who Was Innocent," *New York Times*, 11 February.

Coase, Ronald H. [1960] 1988."The Problem of Social Cost." Pp. 95–156 in *The Firm, the Market, and the Law*. Chicago: University of Chicago Press, 1988. (Reprinted from *Journal of Law and Economics* 3 [1960]: 1–44.)

Colson, Elizabeth. 1974. *Tradition and Contract: The Problem of Order*. Chicago: Aldine.

Couzin, Jennifer. 2002. "Active Polio Virus Baked from Scratch." *Science* 297 (12 July): 174–75.

Dewey, John. [1929] 1960. *The Quest for Certainty: A Study of the Relation of Knowledge and Action*. New York: G. P. Putnam's Sons.

Dickey, Fred. 2000. "Worst-Case Scenario." *Los Angeles Times Magazine*, 25 June, 16–19, 33–34.

Donaldson, Thomas. 1985. "Nuclear Deterrence and Self-Defense." *Ethics* 95 (3): 537–48.

Dwyer, Jim, Peter Neufeld, and Barry Scheck. 2000. *Actual Innocence: Five Days to Execution and Other Dispatches from the Wrongly Convicted*. New York: Doubleday.

Edgeworth, F. Y. 1881. *Mathematical Psychics: An Essay on the Application of Mathematics to the Moral Sciences*. London: C. Kegan Paul.

Feinberg, Joel. 1975. "Rawls and Intuitionism." Pp. 108–24 in Norman Daniels, ed., *Reading Rawls: Critical Studies of A Theory of Justice*. New York: Basic Books.

Fenner, Frank. 1984. "Smallpox, 'the Most Dreadful Scourge of the Human Species': Its Global Spread and Recent Eradication—Part 2." *Medical Journal of Australia* 141 (December 8 and 22): 841–46.

Ferguson, Brian. 1995. *Yanomami Warfare: A Political History*. Santa Fe, NM: School of American Research Press.

Firestone, David. 1999. "DNA Test Brings Freedom, 16 Years after Conviction." *New York Times*, 16 June, sec. A.

Flood, Merrill M. 1958. "Some Experimental Games." *Management Science* 5 (October): 5–26.

Foot, Philippa. [1967] 1978. "The Problem of Abortion and the Doctrine of the Double Effect." Pp. 19–32 in Foot, *Virtues and Vices*. Berkeley and Los Angeles: University of California Press.

Fuller, Lon L. 1969. *The Morality of Law*. Rev. ed. New Haven: Yale University Press.

———. [1969] 1981."Human Interaction and the Law." Pp. 212–46 in *The Principles of Social Order*. Durham, NC: Duke University Press.

Gauthier, David. 1986. *Morals by Agreement*. Oxford: Oxford University Press.

Geertz, Clifford. 2001. "Life among the Anthros." *New York Review of Books* (8 February): 18–22.

Gray, John. 1996. *Isaiah Berlin*. Princeton: Princeton University Press.

Hahn, Frank. 1984. "On the Notion of Equilibrium in Economics." Pp. 43–71 in Frank Hahn, ed., *Equilibrium and Macroeconomics*. Cambridge: MIT Press.

Hallpike, C. R. 1973. "Functionalist Interpretations of Primitive Warfare." *Man* 8 (September): 451–70.

Hardin, Russell. 1976. "Hollow Victory: The Minimum Winning Coalition." *American Political Science Review* 70 (December): 1202–14.

———. 1982a. *Collective Action*. Baltimore: Johns Hopkins University Press.

———. 1982b. "Exchange Theory on Strategic Bases." *Social Science Information* 2 (1982): 251–72.

———. 1984a. "Contracts, Promises, and Arms Control." *Bulletin of the Atomic Scientists* (October): 14–17.

———. 1984b. "Difficulties in the Notion of Economic Rationality." *Social Science Information* 23: 453–67.

———. 1985. "A Rejoinder" (to Richard B. Bilder). *Bulletin of the Atomic Scientists* (April): 53–54.

———. 1986a. "Deterrence and Moral Theory." Pp. 161–93 in David Copp, ed., *Reasoning about War and Strategy in the Nuclear Age: The Philosophers' Point of View. Canadian Journal of Philosophy*, suppl. vol. 12:161–93; reprinted, pp. 35–60 in Kenneth Kipnis and Diana T. Meyers, eds., *Political Realism and International Morality: International Ethics in the Nuclear Age*. Boulder, CO: Westview Press, 1987.

———. 1986b. "Pragmatic Intuitions and Rational Choice." Pp. 27–36 in A. Diekmann and P. Mitter, eds., *Paradoxical Effects of Social Behavior: Essays in Honor of Anatol Rapoport*. Heidelberg: Physica-Verlag.

———. 1987. "Rational Choice Theories." Pp. 67–91 in Terence Ball, ed., *Idioms of Inquiry: Critique and Renewal in Political Science*. Albany: State University of New York Press.

———. 1988. *Morality within the Limits of Reason*. Chicago: University of Chicago Press.

———. 1989. "Ethics and Stochastic Processes." *Social Philosophy and Policy* 7 (Autumn): 69–80.

———. 1990. "Public Choice vs. Democracy." Pp. 184–203 in John W. Chapman, ed., NOMOS 32, *Majorities and Minorities*. New York: New York University Press.

———. 1991. "Hobbesian Political Order." *Political Theory* 19 (May): 156–80.

———. 1992a. "Common Sense at the Foundations." Pp. 143–60 in Bart Schultz, ed., *Essays on Henry Sidgwick*. Cambridge: Cambridge University Press.

———. 1992b. "Determinacy and Rational Choice." Pp. 191–200 in Reinhard Selten, ed., *Rational Interaction: Essays in Honor of John C. Harsanyi*. Berlin: Springer-Verlag.

———. 1993. "Efficiency." Pp. 462–70 in Robert E. Goodin and Philip Pettit, eds., *Companion to Contemporary Political Philosophy*. Oxford: Basil Blackwell.

Hardin, Russell. 1994. "My University's Yacht: Morality and the Rule of Law." Pp. 205–27 in Ian Shapiro, ed., NOMOS 36, *The Rule of Law*. New York: New York University Press.

———. 1995. *One for All: The Logic of Group Conflict*. Princeton: Princeton University Press.

———. 1996. "Magic on the Frontier: The Norm of Efficiency in the Law." *University of Pennsylvania Law Review* 144 (May): 1987–2020.

———. 1998a. "Institutional Commitment: Values or Incentives?" Pp. 419–33 in Avner Ben Ner and Louis Putterman, eds. *Economics, Values, and Organization*. Cambridge: Cambridge University Press.

———. 1998b. "Rational Choice Theory." Pp. 64–75 in Edward Craig, ed., *Routledge Encyclopedia of Philosophy*, vol. 8. London: Routledge.

———. 1998c. "Reasonable Agreement: Political Not Normative." Pp. 137–53 in Paul J. Kelly, ed., *Impartiality, Neutrality, and Justice: Re-reading Brian Barry's* Justice as Impartiality. Edinburg: Edinburg University Press.

———. 1999a. "The Dear Self and Others." *Annual Review of Law and Ethics* 6:211–30.

———. 1999b. "Deliberation: Method Not Theory." Pp. 103–19 in Stephen Macedo, ed., *Deliberative Politics: Essays on Democracy and Disagreement*. Oxford: Oxford University Press.

———. 1999c. "From Bodo Ethics to Distributive Justice." *Ethical Theory and Moral Practice* 2:337–63.

———. 1999d. *Liberalism, Constitutionalism, and Democracy*. Oxford: Oxford University Press.

———. 2001. "The Normative Core of Rational Choice Theory." Pp. 57–74. In Uskali Maki, ed., *The Economic Realm: Studies in the Ontology of Economics*. Cambridge: Cambridge University Press

Harsanyi, John C. 1956. "Approaches to the Bargaining Problem before and after the Theory of Games: A Critical Discussion of Zeuthen's, Hicks', and Nash's Theories." *Econometrica* 24: 144–57.

———. 1977. *Rational Behavior and Bargaining Equilibrium in Games and Social Situations*. Cambridge: Cambridge University Press.

Harsanyi, John C., and Reinhard Selten. 1988. *A General Theory of Equilibrium Selection in Games*. Cambridge: MIT Press.

Hart, H.L.A. 1961. *The Concept of Law*. Oxford: Oxford University Press.

———. 1979. "Between Utility and Rights." Pp. 198–222 in *Essays in Jurisprudence and Philosophy*. Oxford: Oxford University Press.

Hayek, Friedrich. 1948a. "Economics and Knowledge." Pp. 33–56 in *Individualism and Economic Order*. Chicago: University of Chicago Press.

———. 1948b. "The Use of Knowledge in Society." Pp. 77–91 in *Individualism and Economic Order*. Chicago: University of Chicago Press.

———. 1960a. *The Constitution of Liberty*. Chicago: University of Chicago Press.

———. 1960b. "Why I Am Not a Conservative." Pp. 397–411 in *The Constitution of Liberty*. Chicago: University of Chicago Press.

Herbert, Bob. 1999. "How Many Innocent Prisoners?" *New York Times* (18 July), Op-Ed page.

Herman, Barbara. 1993. *The Practice of Moral Judgment*. Cambridge: Harvard University Press.

Hobbes, Thomas. [1642] 1983. *De Cive*. Edited by Howard Warrender. Oxford: Oxford University Press.

————. [1651] 1968. *Leviathan*. Edited by C. B. Macpherson. London: Penguin. Originally published in London by Andrew Cooke. (There are many editions. I give chapter and page numbers in the Macpherson edition and page numbers in [brackets] in the original edition.)

Hopkins, Donald R. 2000. *The Greatest Killer: Smallpox in History*. Chicago: University of Chicago Press.

Hume, David. [1739–40] 1978. *A Treatise of Human Nature* 2nd ed. Edited by L. A. Selby-Bigge and P. H. Nidditch. Oxford: Oxford University Press.

————. [1742] 1985. "Of the Independency of Parliament." Pp. 42–46 in Eugene F. Miller, ed., *David Hume: Essays Moral, Political, and Literary*. Indianapolis: Liberty Classics.

————. [1748] 1985. "Of the Original Contract." Pp. 465–87 in *David Hume: Essays Moral, Political, and Literary*. Indianapolis: Liberty Classics.

————. [1751] 1975. *An Enquiry Concerning the Principles of Morals*. Pp. 167–323 in Hume, *Enquiries*, ed. L. A. Selby-Bigge and P. H. Nidditch, 3rd ed. Oxford: Oxford University Press.

Jeffrey, Richard C. 1983. *The Logic of Decision*. 2nd ed. Chicago: University of Chicago Press.

Kant, Immanuel. [1797] 1909. "On a Supposed Right to Tell Lies from Benevolent Motives." Pp. 361–65 in Thomas Kingsmill Abbott, ed. and trans., *Kant's* Critique of Practical Reason *and other works on the Theory of Ethics*. 6th ed. London: Longman's.

————. [1785] 1964. *Groundwork of the Metaphysics of Morals*. Translated by H. J. Paton. New York: Harper and Row.

————. 1963. *Lectures on Ethics*. Translated by Louis Infield. New York: Harper and Row.

Kirman, A. P. 1987. "Pareto as an Economist." Pp. 804–9 in John Eatwell, Murray Milgate, and Peter Newman, eds., *The New Palgrave: A Dictionary of Economics*, vol. 3. London: Macmillan.

Koshland, Daniel E., Jr. 1985. "Benefits, Risks, Vaccines, and the Courts." *Science*, 227 (15 March): 1289.

Kreps, David M., Paul Milgrom, John Roberts, and Robert Wilson. 1982. "Rational Cooperation in a Finitely Repeated Prisoner's Dilemma." *Journal of Economic Theory* 27:245–52.

Ledyard, John O. 1995. "Public Goods: A Survey of Experimental Research." Pp. 111–94 in Al Roth and John Kagel, eds., *Handbook of Experimental Economics*. Princeton: Princeton University Press.

Leijonhufvud, Axel. 1995. "The Individual, the Market, and the Industrial Division of Labor." Pp. 61–78 in Carlo Mongardini, ed. *L'Individuo e il mercato*. Rome: Bulzoi.

Locke, John. [1690] 1988. *Two Treatises of Government*. Cambridge: Cambridge University Press.

Lovinger, Caitlin. 1999. "Death Row's Living Alumni" and "Life after Death Row," *New York Times* (22 August), sec. 4.

Luce, R. Duncan, and Howard Raiffa. 1957. *Games and Decisions*. New York: Wiley.

Lyons, David. 2000. "The Moral Opacity of Utilitarianism." Pp. 105–20, in Brad Hooker, Elinor Mason, and Dale E. Miller, eds., *Morality, Rules, and Consequences: A Critical Reader*. Edinburgh: Edinburgh University Press.

Mann, Charles C. 2001. "Anthropological Warfare." *Science* 291 (19 January): 416–21.

Marx, Karl. 1906. *Capital*. Translated by Ernest Untermann. New York: Random House.

Matson, W. I. [1954] 1967. "Kant as Casuist." Pp. 331–36 in Robert Paul Wolff, ed., *Kant: A Collection of Critical Essays*. Garden City, NY: Doubleday Anchor.

Moore, G. E. 1903. *Principia Ethica*. Cambridge: Cambridge University Press.

Morgenbesser, Sidney and Edna Ullmann-Margalit. 1977. "Picking and Choosing." *Social Research* 44 (Winter): 757–85.

Mueller, Dennis. 1989. *Public Choice II*. Cambridge: Cambridge University Press.

Nagel, Thomas. 1977. "The Fragmentation of Value." Pp. 128–41 in Nagel, *Mortal Questions*. Cambridge: Cambridge University Press, 1979.

———. 1998. "Concealment and Exposure." *Philosophy and Public Affairs* 27:3–30.

Nozick, Robert. 1974. *Anarchy, the State, and Utopia*. New York: Basic Books.

Nyberg, David. 1993. *The Varnished Truth: Truth Telling and Deceiving in Ordinary Life*. Chicago: University of Chicago Press.

Okun, Arthur M. 1975. *Equality and Efficiency: The Big Tradeoff*. Washington, DC: Brookings Institution.

Paley, William. [1785] 1978. *The Principles of Moral and Political Philosophy*. New York: Garland.

Pareto, Vilfredo. [1927] 1971. *Manual of Political Economy* (translation by Ann S. Schwier from the French edition) New York: Kelley.

Pigou, A. C. [1920] 1932. *The Economics of Welfare*. 4th ed. London: Macmillan.

Polinsky, A. Mitchell. 1989. *An Introduction to Law and Economics*. 2nd ed. Boston: Little, Brown.

Pollard, Rebecca. 2000. "Crime Genes: A DNA Mismatch Raises Fears." *Technology Review* (May/June): 29.

Posner, Richard A. 1980. "The Value of Wealth: A Comment on Dworkin and Kronman." *Journal of Legal Studies* 9:243–52.

———. 1981. *The Economics of Justice*. Cambridge: Harvard University Press.

———. 1992. *Economic Analysis of Law*. 4th edition. Boston: Little, Brown.

Preston, Richard. 1999. "The Demon in the Freezer." *New Yorker* (12 July): 44–61.

Pufendorf, Samuel. [1672] 1717. *On the Law of Nature and Nations in Eight Books*. London: R. Sare et al.

Radner, Roy. 1980. "Collusive Behavior in Noncooperative Epsilon-Equilibria of Oligopolies with Long but Finite Lives." *Journal of Economic Theory* 22:136–54.

Rawls, John. 1955. "Two Concepts of Rules." *Philosophical Review* 67 (April): 3–32.

———. 1958. "Justice As Fairness." *Philosophical Review* 67 (April): 164–94.

———. [1971] 1999. *A Theory of Justice*. Rev. ed. Cambridge: Harvard University Press.

————. 1996. *Political Liberalism*. New York: Columbia University Press.

Raz, Joseph. 1986. *The Morality of Freedom*. Oxford: Oxford University Press.

Riker, William H. 1962. *The Theory of Political Coalitions*. New Haven: Yale University Press.

Roberts, Leslie. 1988. "Change in Polio Strategy?" *Science* 240 (27 May): 1145.

Samuelson, Paul. 1974. "Complementarity: An Essay on the 40th Anniversary of the Hicks-Allen Revolution in Demand Theory." *Journal of Economic Literature* 12:1255–89.

Scanlon, Thomas M. 1999. *What We Owe to Each Other*. Cambridge: Harvard University Press.

Schumpeter, Joseph A. [1942] 1950. *Capitalism, Socialism, and Democracy*. 3rd ed. New York: Harper.

Scitovsky, Tibor. 1952. *Welfare and Competition*. London: George Allen and Unwin.

Selten, Reinhard. 1985. "Comment." Pp. 77–85 in Kenneth J. Arrow and Seppo Honkapohja, eds., *Frontiers of Economics*. Oxford: Basil Blackwell.

Sen, Amartya. 1985. "Well-Being, Agency, and Freedom: The Dewey Lectures, 1984." *Journal of Philosophy* 82:169–221.

————. 1999. *Development as Freedom*. New York: Knopf.

Shalala, Donna. 1999. "Smallpox: Setting the Research Agenda." *Science* 285 (13 August): 1011.

Sidgwick, Henry. 1907. *The Methods of Ethics*. 7th ed. London: Macmillan.

Slote, Michael. 1985. *Common-Sense Morality and Consequentialism*. Boston: Routledge and Kegan Paul.

————. 1989. *Beyond Optimizing: A Study of Rational Choice*. Cambridge: Harvard University Press.

Smith, R. Jeffrey. 1984. "Missile Deployments Roil Europe." *Science* 223 (27 January): 373.

Sorensen, Roy A. 1988. *Blindspots*. Oxford: Oxford University Press.

Sorrenson, E. R. 1972. "Socio-Ecological Change among the Fore of New Guinea." *Current Anthropology* 13:349–84.

Stigler, George J. [1959] 1965. "The Politics of Political Economists." Pp. 51–65 in Stigler, *Essays in the History of Economics*. Chicago: University of Chicago Press.

————. 1978. "Wealth, and Possibly Liberty." *Journal of Legal Studies* 7:213–17.

————. 1982. "The Adoption of the Marginal Utility Theory." Pp. 72–85 in Stigler, *The Economist as Preacher and Other Essays*. Chicago: University of Chicago Press.

Sun, Marjorie. 1985. "The Vexing Problems of Vaccine Compensation." *Science* 227 (1 March): 1012–14.

Thompson, Jennifer. 2000. "I Was Certain, but I Was Wrong." *New York Times* (18 June), Op-Ed.

Thomson, Judith Jarvis. 1986. "Imposing Risks." Pp. in 173–91. In Thomson, *Rights, Restitution, and Risk*. Cambridge: Harvard University Press.

Tierney, Patrick. 2000. *Darkness in El Dorado: How Scientists and Journalists Devastated the Amazon*. New York: Norton.

von Neumann, John, and Oskar Morgenstern. [1944] 1953. *Theory of Games and Economic Behavior*. 3rd ed. Princeton: Princeton University Press.

Waddington, C. H. [1960] 1967. *The Ethical Animal*. Chicago: University of Chicago Press.

Wade, Betsy. 1999. "Saving Lives in the Air." *New York Times* (9 May), sec. 5.

Williams, Bernard. 1972. *Morality: An Introduction to Ethics*. New York: Harper.

Winstanley, Gerrard. [1652] 1973. *The Law of Freedom in a Platform; or, True Magistracy Restored*. New York: Shocken.

Wong, Kate. 2001. "Fighting the Darkness in El Dorado." *Scientific American* (March): 26–28.

INDEX